P9-DFP-650

Boredom
BLASTERS

Maple Tree Press Inc.
51 Front Street East, Suite 200, Toronto, Ontario M5E 1B3
www.mapletreepress.com

Text © 2004 Helaine Becker
Illustrations © 2004 Claudia Dávila

All rights reserved. No part of this book may be reproduced or copied in any form without written consent from the publisher.

Distributed in Canada by Raincoast Books
9050 Shaughnessy Street, Vancouver, British Columbia V6P 6E5

Distributed in the United States by Publishers Group West
1700 Fourth Street, Berkeley, California 94710

We acknowledge the financial support of the Canada Council for the Arts, the Ontario Arts Council, the Government of Canada through the Book Publishing Industry Development Program (BPIDP), and the Government of Ontario through the Ontario Media Development Corporation's Book Initiative for our publishing activities.

Dedication
For Michael and Andrew—the two best kids I know!

Cataloguing in Publication Data

Becker, Helaine, 1961-
    Boredom blasters : brain bogglers, awesome activities, cool comics, tasty treats, and more— / by Helaine Becker ; illustrated by Claudia Dávila.

ISBN 1-897066-02-3 (bound).—ISBN 1-897066-03-1 (pbk.)

    1. Amusements—Juvenile literature. I. Dávila, Claudia II. Title.

GV1203.B38 2004   j790.1'922   C2003-904689-3

Design & art direction: Claudia Dávila
Illustrations: Claudia Dávila

Printed in China

A   B   C   D   E   F

The activities in this book have been tested and are safe when conducted as instructed. The author and publisher accept no responsibility for any damage caused or sustained by the use or misuse of ideas or material featured in *Boredom Blasters*.

ST. BERNADETTE SCHOOL - RESOURCE CENTRE

Boredom BLASTERS

Brain Bogglers, Awesome Activities, Cool Comics, Tasty Treats, and More...

WRITTEN BY

HELAINE BECKER

ILLUSTRATED BY

CLAUDIA DÁVILA

MAPLE
TREE
PRESS

CONTENTS

Awesome Activities

Yummy Things to Make and Eat

Brain Bogglers

Games, Games, Games

Last but Not Least...

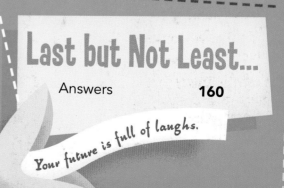

Your future is full of laughs.

YE OLDE HOLE IN
YER HAND TRICK

Awesome

YE OLDE MINI HOTDOG TRICK

Activities

MONSTER
FOOTPRINTS

BREAD BAG TAG RACERS

Silly Kid

Ye Olde Silly Spoon Trick

Only the nose knows for sure
how this wacky trick works.

1 Find a clean metal spoon.

2 Exhale hard through your mouth onto
the bowl of the spoon.

3 Gently balance the bowl of the spoon
on the tip of your nose with the handle
hanging down.

4 See how long you and your friends
can keep the spoons in place.

5 Look in the mirror and ask yourselves,
"Why are we doing this?"

Tricks

Ye Olde Keep Your Nose Clean Drinking Trick

Challenge your friends to drink a sip of water without putting their noses inside the glass. Can't be done? Here's how (it's a good idea to do this outside or over a sink):

1. Fill a plastic cup with water.
2. Bend over the glass (see illustration).
3. Put your lips on the *far* side of the glass.
4. Tip the glass slightly away from your body.
5. Slurp up the water.

Ye Olde Silly String Challenge

This trick will have your friends tied up in knots. Give them a string that measures about 30 cm (12 in.) long. Challenge them to tie it in a knot, *without letting go of either end*. Here's the naughty (knotty) secret:

1. Place the string on a table.
2. Cross your arms the way you usually do when you are refusing to do something completely unreasonable.
3. Without uncrossing your arms, grab both ends of the string in your hands. Unless you are double-jointed, you might need to grab one end at a time.
4. Uncross your arms, pulling the string through. The string will automatically tie itself into a knot!

Left hand over

Right hand under

Silly Kid Tricks II

Ye Olde Silly Stick 'em Up Challenge

Can't get someone to leave you alone? Stick 'em to a wall and leave them there for a while so you can get some peace.

1 Challenge your friend to stand with his head, his shoulder, and one side of his foot pressed tightly against the wall.

2 Have him try and lift his outside foot off the ground without moving any body part away from the wall. He won't be able to—no way, no how.

Ye Olde Silly Chair Trick

Similar to the Stick 'em Up Challenge, but your victim looks even sillier in this trick.

1 Place a chair against the wall. Any ordinary, straight-backed chair will do.

2 Challenge your friend to pick up the chair and bring it to you. Of course, your friend will agree to this "simple" challenge.

3 Now tell her that there are two very minor conditions. One: she must stand with her feet about 15 cm (6 in.) in front of the chair. And two: she must keep the top of her head touching the wall (see illustration). Looks easy enough, doesn't it?

4 Let her get herself into this position. Giggle. Then say, "Okay, bring the chair over."

5 Forget about carrying the chair—your friend won't even be able to stand up straight. Her head will seem like it's stuck to the wall!

6 Once you stop laughing at your friend in this position, try it yourself.

WHY DOES THIS SILLY KID TRICK WORK?

Easy peasy—it all has to do with your center of gravity. Gravity is pulling down on you all the time. Otherwise you'd fly off into space like a helium-filled balloon. Gravity works by exerting a force on your body. The force is centered on a single point in your body, known as your "center of gravity," located in the lower abdomen. When you bend over with your head to the wall, and hold the chair, you shift your center of gravity. Now, it is centered somewhere in the middle of your chest. No wonder you can't stand up! The whole earth is working against you, pulling your upper body down, down, down....You can shift back to your normal center of gravity by pushing against the wall with your hands. Holding the chair, however, prevents you from doing this. As long as you've got the chair in your hands, you are one stuck puppy.

Silly Kid Tricks III

Ye Olde Mysterious Finger Trick

In this fun trick, you can really fool your brain into not knowing which of your own fingers is which!

1. Hold your arms straight out in front of you.

2. Turn your hands away from each other so both palms are facing out.

3. Cross one arm over the other so now your palms are facing each other, and clasp your fingers together.

4. Without letting go, bring both hands toward you, turning them over so that your knuckles are facing you.

5. With your hands in this position, have a friend point to one of your fingers. (Make sure they do not actually touch the finger, just point to it.)

6. Move the finger you saw them point to. Chances are you will move the wrong one!

Ye Olde Hole in Yer Hand Trick

People never quit getting a kick out of this old favorite.

1 Find an empty toilet paper or paper towel roll, or roll a piece of paper into a tube shape.

2 Holding it in your left hand, bring the tube up to your left eye.

3 With your palm toward your face, touch your open right hand to the right side of the tube about halfway down.

4 Keeping both eyes open, you should see a perfect hole going straight through your hand!

Ye Olde Mini Hotdog Trick

1 Hold your two index fingers (the fingers beside your thumbs) horizontally in front of you, about 5 cm (2 in.) in front of your nose. The fingertips should almost, but not quite, touch.

2 Look *at* your fingertips, then look *past* your fingertips. Can you see a mini hotdog floating mysteriously between your fingertips? Yum.

Your Friends Are
Soooo
punny!

Which friend has trouble standing up straight?

Ilene.

Who is your sweetest friend?

Candy.

Which is your friend most likely to wind up in jail?

Rob.

Which one of your friends has a lot to offer?

Rich.

Which of your friends loves to bungee jump?

Cliff.

Which one of your friends is crazy about the beach?

Sandy.

Which one of your friends is going to be a great lawyer?

Sue.

Which of your friends is a terrific athlete?

Jim.

Which one of your friends lets other people walk all over him?

Matt.

Which of your friends loves hamburgers?

Patty.

Which one of your friends would probably taste the best?

Stu.

magic money

These extra-easy magic tricks are extra-fun.
For best results, use your brother's allowance!

SUPER-ABRACADABRA HINT

Practice all of these tricks ahead of time in front of a mirror. This way, you will be able to see how they look to your audience— totally awesome or pretty amateurish. Keep practicing until they all are awesome!

There's the Rub

Take two quarters and quickly slide them back and forth, between your finger and thumb. If you do this fast enough, it will look like there are three coins in your fingers. Ask your buddies, "How many coins do I have?" Astound them when you show them one of the three coins has disappeared!

Multiplying Money

In this trick, your money will seem to magically multiply by ten!

(1) Hold a nickel between the thumb and index finger of your right hand as shown.

(2) Carefully place two quarters against the back of the nickel as shown. The nickel should face out, with the two quarters sideways behind it. When you hold the nickel facing your audience, the quarters will be invisible.

(3) Briefly cover your right hand with your left hand to conceal your magical moves from the audience.

Nickel in front, two quarters hidden behind

Left hand flashes in front of right

(4) While your right hand is hidden behind your left, gently collapse the coins into a stack, and push the nickel underneath the quarters.

Collapse the nickel onto the quarters

(5) Say: Ta-dah! Hiding the nickel behind one of the quarters, hold up the coins to show the audience that you now have fifty cents instead of a nickel.

THESE INSTRUCTIONS WORK THE SAME FOR LEFTIES.

magic money 11

Face Up to It!

Astound your friends by saying you have "mirror" pennies. They like to mirror each other's behavior. Here's how:

1 Place twelve pennies on a table. Make sure six pennies are heads up and six are heads down.

2 Explain to people that even if you take away some of the pennies, they will stay "in sync" with the ones on the table. Point out that there are equal numbers of heads and tails showing. Tell them that, whichever pennies you remove, the ones in your hands will magically "change faces" so they match what is still showing on the table. So, for example, if you remove six tails and leave six heads, they will miraculously change into heads while they are in your hands.

3 Turn your back to the table. Direct your audience to slide the pennies around to mix them up, *without turning any over.*

4 Keeping your back to the table so people don't suspect you of cheating, carefully reach behind you and slide six pennies from the table into your hand. Carefully stack them in your hand. *Make sure none of the pennies turn over.*

18

6 Direct the audience to cover the remaining pennies with their hands.

7 Turn over the entire stack of pennies together in your hand, so that now all of the pennies that were heads are tails, and vice versa.

8 Place the pennies with the new side up on the table.

5 Explain to your audience that now that the pennies are in your hand, they are changing to match the ones left on the table. Point out also that at no time have you seen the pennies, and you have no idea which pennies were removed from the table.

9 Ask your audience to uncover the pennies. Ta-dah! They show exactly the same number of heads and tails as in your batch.

Wow, it's magic!

magic money III

Headstand

Ask your audience if they've ever seen a president, prime minister, or queen do a headstand!

1. Hold a bill so the president, prime minister, or queen's picture is facing the audience.

2. Fold the bill in half lengthwise, bringing the top edge toward the audience and down.

3. Fold the bill in half again, bringing the right side toward the audience and across to the left edge.

4. Repeat step 3, bringing the right side of the bill toward the audience and across to the left edge. The bill should now be folded in eighths. Make sure your audience is aware that at no time are you turning the bill over.

5. Unfold the bill with your **right** hand holding the left corner (see * step 4) of the folded bill. With your **left** hand, unfold by pulling the corner closest to you out to the right.

6. Using your **left** hand, unfold by pulling the corner closest to you (see • step 5) out to the left.

7. Lift the **bottom** edge of the bill on the side facing the audience. Ta-dah! The president, prime minister, or queen is doing a headstand!

① (AUDIENCE POINT OF VIEW)

(STEPS 2-6 MAGICIAN'S POINT OF VIEW)

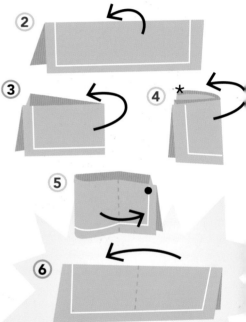

⑦ (AUDIENCE POINT OF VIEW)

Ta-dah!

When You've Hot, You've Hot

Can you figure out which coin your audience has selected when your back was turned?
Of course you can, because when you're hot, you're hot!

1. Place three identical coins on a table.

2. Turn your back and ask someone in your audience to pick up a coin while you are not looking.

3. Ask them to "put their vibes" into the coin by thinking hard about magic, sports, whatever is special to them while they hold it.

4. Keep them holding the coin for about **30 seconds**, saying, "You're not thinking hard enough, c'mon, put your vibes into that coin!" Keep your back turned the whole time so no one calls you a cheater later.

5. When 30 seconds or more has elapsed, have them place the coin back on the table exactly where it was.

6. Explain that you will identify their coin by feeling for the "vibes."

7. Touch each coin in turn. The coin that was selected should feel warmer than the others, since it will have absorbed some body heat from your friend's hands.

8. Select the warm coin and ask if it's the one.

9. Bow.

21

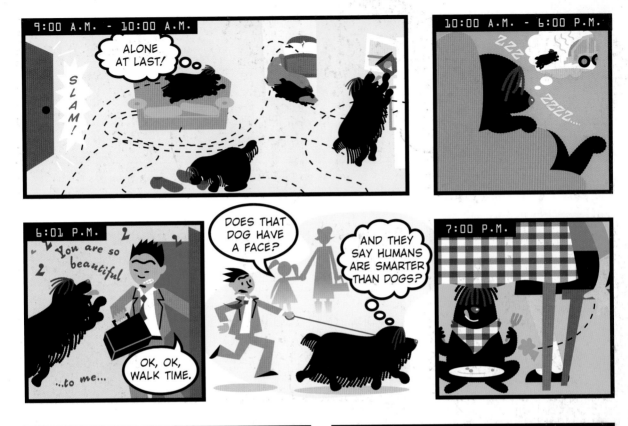

23

MYSTICAL WHEEL OF FORTUNE

Ever wonder what other people think of you? Or what your future holds? Find out with this nifty fortune-telling device. This one is for fun, but it's based on the Mystic Wheel, an ancient device used by medieval scientists.

① Lay the tracing paper over the wheel at right. Trace along all dotted lines of the template (outer edge and small circles).

② Carefully cut the wheel out of the tracing paper. Using your pencil, poke holes through the small circles. Make the holes as large as the circles you've drawn.

③ Lay the tracing paper onto your craft paper. You might want to use small pieces of tape to hold it in place.

④ Carefully draw around the outline of the wheel onto the craft paper. Draw circles through the little holes.

⑤ Cut out your Mystical Wheel from the craft paper. Repeat step 2 to poke holes through the craft paper.

⑥ Draw the one large and seven small arrows onto the craft paper in their proper spots.

⑦ Decorate the Mystical Wheel of Fortune with colors and symbols that are meaningful to you and only you. While you are decorating the wheel, concentrate on your inner self, the part of you that makes you unique. Either that, or think about what you're going to have for dinner. The choice is yours.

Now you're ready to find answers to those burning questions. Clear your mind, then follow the directions on the next pages to discover who you are, and what your future holds.

TRACING TEMPLATE

YOU'LL NEED
tracing paper
pencil
scissors
craft paper
tape
markers or
crayons

Who You Are

Use the grid at right to find out what other people think of you. Yes, of course they think you're wonderful. But what *else* do they think? You could always ask them, but this is way more fun.

★ Choose a number from one to twelve to begin your search. For inspiration, use your age, a number based on the day of your birth, or any number with meaning to you.

★ You can only use this grid to find out about any one person once during the year. If you ask about any person more than once in a year, it might give you a false reading.

★ When you have selected your number, place the large arrow on the Mystical Wheel so it points to that number on the grid. Your reading will appear in the windows in a clockwise direction beginning with the first letter to the left of the small arrow.

27

Your Future

Use this grid to find out what may be in store for you in the years ahead.

★ To begin your search, select a card at random from a playing deck. If you select a King or a Joker, the fortune grid will not work for you at this time. If you select a Jack, use eleven. If you select a Queen, use twelve.

★ Place the wheel so that the large arrow points to your magic number (number on playing card) on the Future grid.

★ Your answer will appear clockwise in the windows, starting to the left of the small arrow.

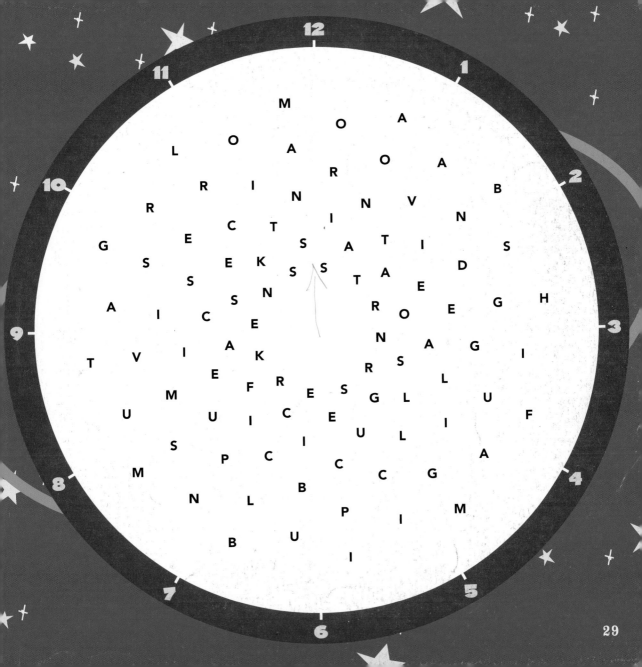

29

Palm Reading
for beginners

The ancient art of palm reading was used by very cheap—er, wise—practitioners to discover secrets such as how to make money (for the fortune teller, that is). Use the key at right to find out what your paws may reveal about you and your friends.

head line

children lines

life line

heart line

writer's fork

line of fame

fate line

Where do fortune tellers like to vacation? Wherever there are palm trees.

LIFE LINE

LONG AND UNBROKEN — You have robust health.

BROKEN, with line continuing further away from thumb — You were shy when you were younger, and are now more outgoing.

BROKEN, with overlapping lines — There will be a big change in your life, but it will go smoothly.

HEART LINE

ZIG ZAG "chain" at outside of hand — You are a flirt.

DEEP AND DARK — You have a loyal, loving nature.

FAINT — You are shy in matters of love.

FORKED LINES leading *up* from heart line near thumb — You will have many loves.

FORKED LINES leading *down* from heart line near thumb — You are ruled by your head, not your heart.

HEAD LINE

DEEP AND DARK — You are logical; you "use your head."

FAINT — You like to please others.

LONG AND STRAIGHT — You have many skills.

CROSSED WITH VERTICAL LINE — You will face opposition: be firm in your beliefs.

FATE LINE

STARTS LOW IN HAND — You have had one goal since early childhood.

STRAIGHT, DARK LINE — You have determination to reach your goals.

FATE LINE CROSSES HEAD LINE — You will almost certainly achieve your goals.

NO FATE LINE, faint or curved line — You will change paths many times in life.

CHILDREN LINES

Indicates how many children you might have.

LINE OF FAME

If present, success will come with much fame.

WRITER'S FORK

If present, you have writing ability.

Palm Reading for Chimps

And now, for the first time, fortune-telling tips for chimpanzees everywhere.

LIFE LINE
The longer the line, the greater the number of bananas you will eat in your life.

FATE LINE
Shows if you will ever be satisfied with the number of bananas you have.

HEAD LINE
Indicates how often you think about bananas.

HEART LINE
How much you love bananas.

COUNT 'EM LINES
Best number of bananas to have for breakfast.

PRIMATE'S FORK
If present, mash all bananas with a fork.

LINE OF FAME
You will become famous for sharing bananas.

BARS CROSSING ANY LINE
Beware of zookeepers promising lifetime supply of bananas.

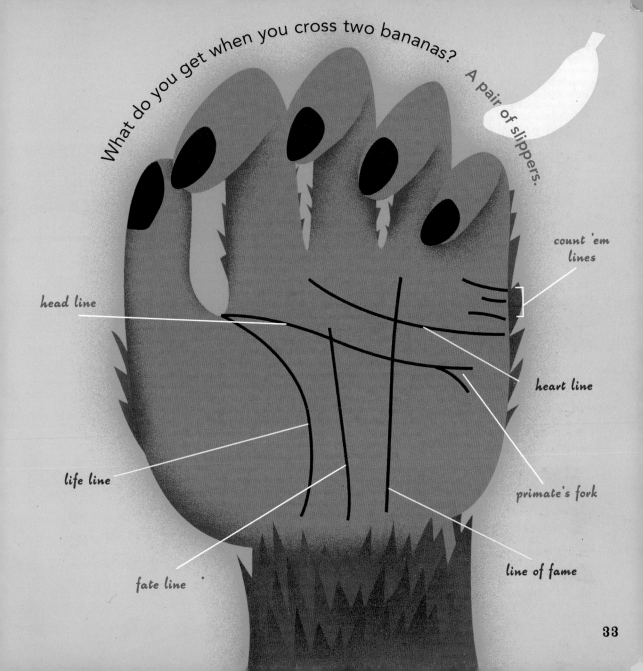

What do you get when you cross two bananas? A pair of slippers.

head line

count 'em lines

life line

heart line

fate line

primate's fork

line of fame

Fortune BINGO

Be the funkiest fortune teller simply by using our handy dandy Fortune-for-All-Occasions table at right. Have your victim, er, friend ask any question and choose a number from one to ten.

Look up her number in the lefthand column and then read across the row for the answer. For example, if she asks "What will I be when I grow up?" and chooses the number seven, you can let her know you see belly dancing in her future. If she asks "Who will I marry?" choose the answer from the Name column that corresponds to her number.

Sample Questions

What will I be when I grow up? (Career)

Who will I marry? (Name)

What will I do for fun? (Activity)

What will be my biggest achievement? (Activity)

Where will I live? (Place)

How old will I be when I
...marry? (Number)
...strike it rich? (Number)
...do an ollie? (Number)

How many boyfriends/girlfriends will I have? (Number)

Who is in love with me? (Name)

How will I become famous? (Activity)

#	CAREER	NAME	PLACE	ACTIVITY	NUMBER
1	chicken wrangler	(pop star)	inside a fiery volcano	playing poker	12
2	shoe lacer	(a fun classmate)	the middle of nowhere	staying awake at the opera	25
3	nuclear physicist	(the U.S. president)	Paris	saving the universe	2
4	clown	(a brainy classmate)	under a rock	training monkeys	66
5	professional dog walker	(your tallest classmate)	a ski chalet in Antarctica	ordering pepperoni pizza with extra cheese and anchovies	99
6	pearl diver	(childhood friend)	Kalamazoo, Michigan	accepting the Nobel Peace Prize	24
7	belly dancer	(popular teacher)	your grandmother's house	balancing on one foot for 37 days, 3 hours, and 7 seconds	45
8	heavy metal guitar player	(school principal)	a carwash	swimming with sharks	5
9	lion tamer	(movie star)	Brazil	surviving grade 8	81
10	screwdriver repair technician	(sports star)	the moon	shooting spaghetti out of your nose when you laugh	15

You can create your own twisted questions and fortunes for the funniest "readings" ever.

fire-breathing DRAGON

Forget about gerbils and fish. What all kids really want is their very own Mean 'n' Nasty, Fire-Breathing, Bad Mood-Having, Totally Impressive Pet. There'd be no more teasing in the schoolyard, that's for sure! Follow these directions to make your own fire-breathing dragon bookmark.

YOU'LL NEED

ruler

scissors

colored pencils

craft paper in your favorite pale shade

felt tip markers or food coloring

glass jar

water

Chivalry Limerick

There once was a dragon so chivalrous
He thought toasted princesses frivolous
And though he was teased
He ate what he pleased
And resisted becoming carnivorous.

1 Carefully cut the craft paper into a strip about 4 cm (1 1/2 in.) wide and about 15 cm (6 in.) long. This will be your bookmark.

2 Using the colored pencils, draw a dragon with its mouth open. It looks best to draw it length-wise starting at the bottom with the open mouth pointing up.

3 When you are satisfied with your drawing, grab your felt tip markers or the food coloring. Dab different colored dots in the dragon's mouth and just above the snout. Red, orange, and purple look totally cool together.

4 Fill the glass jar with about 1 cm (1/2 in.) of water.

5 Stand the bookmark in the water with the bottom edge standing in the puddle.

6 Be patient. The water will gradually seep up the bookmark (the magic of capillary action*). When it hits the colored dots, they will begin to spread into a fiery mass.

7 When the dragon's breath looks stinky and flaming, remove the bookmark from the water and lay it flat on a paper towel or newspaper. Allow it to dry before using.

*WHAT IS CAPILLARY ACTION?

Water likes to hang out with other substances rather than stick to itself. It's a friendly element. The force that holds water to things like paper and plastic is called adhesion. The force of adhesion is so strong that it can even overcome gravity. That's why the water can travel up the bookmark—it is adhering to the paper and overcoming gravity. As the water passes through the dots you made with your marker or food coloring, the water dissolves the colors, carrying them along with it on its upward journey. The result? Very wet flames.

FURRY
Abominable
SNOWMAN

RAAAH!

Bigfoot. Yeti. Abominable Snowman. Call it what you will, this fuzzy, wacky critter really does exist. Honest. You can see it with your own eyes.

Wouldn't it be "cool" (get it?) if you could have your own fuzzy Abominable Snowman? Well, it's pretty easy, and pretty nifty too, if you follow the instructions below.

1 Lay the tracing paper over the Abominable Snowman template shown on this page. Trace over the dotted lines.

2 Carefully cut the snowman out of the tracing paper.

3 Lay the tracing paper onto your cardboard. You might want to use small pieces of tape to hold it in place.

4 Using your pencil, carefully draw around the outline of the snowman onto the cardboard.

5 Carefully cut out the snowman from the cardboard.

6 Fold the cardboard through the center along the solid line so your snowman stands on all four feet. Place it like this in the pie plate.

YOU'LL NEED

Abominable Snowman template

tracing paper   pencil

scissors   cardboard

tape   pie plate

saucepan or microwavable bowl

500 mL (2 cups) hot water

90 mL (6 tbsp.) borax
(available in a pharmacy or supermarket;
also called boric acid)

7 In a saucepan on the stove, or in a bowl in the microwave, heat 500 mL (2 cups) water to just below the boiling point. (Ask an adult to help you with this.) Remove from heat.

8 Add the borax, 15 mL (1 tbsp.) at a time to the hot water. Stir until the borax dissolves. Keep adding borax to the water until all of the 90 mL (6 tbsp.) is dissolved.

9 Carefully pour the borax solution into the pie plate. It should puddle around your snowman's feet.

10 Place your pie plate in a safe place where it will not be jiggled or disturbed.

11 Over the next few days, crystals should form on your snowman, making a white shaggy coat.

12 When all the water in the plate has evaporated and your snowman is dry, carefully remove it from the plate and stand it on its hind legs. Practice making silly roaring sounds for it.

What steps should you take if you see a dangerous Yeti on your travels?

Very large ones.

What do Yetis drink on top of Mount Everest?

High tea.

How did the Yeti feel when it had the flu?

Abominable.

What do you call a Yeti in a phone booth?

Stuck.

Abominable JOKES

What do Abominable Snowmen call their kids?

Chill-dren.

Where do Abominable Snowmen go to dance?

To snow balls.

What do you give a seasick Yeti?

Lots and lots of room.

Where do you find wild Yetis?

It depends where you left them.

What do you get if you cross a Yeti with a kangaroo?

A fur coat with big pockets.

Why was the Abominable Snowman's dog called Frost?

Because Frost bites.

When should you feed Yeti milk to a baby?

When it's a baby Yeti.

What did one Abominable Snowman say to the other?

I'm afraid I just don't believe in people.

How does a Yeti get to work?

By icicle.

Where are Yetis found?

They're so big they're hardly ever lost.

What do you get if you cross an airplane with an Abominable Snowman?

A jumbo jeti.

41

DAILY
~25¢~

The

MONSTER

Mysterious footprints appeared across our town yesterday, in an incident officials are calling "Really, really weird." The giant footprints appear to be those of an extinct *plesiomonsterohelpusasaurus*, a fierce predator with really bad breath.

Milton Cherrypit, Director of the City Museum, says, "If those giant footprints are what I think they are, I'm outta here!" The mayor, Hernanda Duckit, could not be reached for comment, although her aides said she was last seen packing a very big suitcase.

The huge footprints have been spotted on sidewalks all across the city. A particularly good set of footprints can be seen at Joe the Butcher's, where the monster apparently stopped to make a wish list.

City residents are told that if they see any large unidentified footprints, they should not panic and should call the City Help Line, press 1, then wait for the beep before screaming hysterically.

MONSTER FOOT- PRiNTS

Is there a Yeti loose in your area? Everyone will think so after you've made these giant Monster Footprint stampers and used them to leave mystifying tracks all over town!

YOU'LL NEED

large pieces of cardboard or styrofoam

scissors

pencil

cloth strips about 15 cm (6 in.)

tape

washable tempera paint

paint pan

1. Draw an outline of a really big left foot on the cardboard or styrofoam. (It can be a giant human foot, or something like a dinosaur foot—your choice.) Cut out.

2. Place cutout of your really big left foot on the cardboard or styrofoam and trace around it to make another foot exactly like the first. Cut it out and turn it over. Ta-dah! Now you have a really big right foot.

3. Using the tape, attach both ends of the cloth strips to the top sides of the feet to make handles. This will make it easier to lift your stampers after you have stamped.

4. Wait until the coast is clear so no one sees you in action. It would also be a good idea to make sure it's not about to rain soon.

5. Wear old clothes. Fill a paint pan with paint. Make sure you have your parents' permission.

6. Carefully dip the bottom of your left foot stamper into the paint pan. Try not to let paint squish up onto the top, or your prints will get messy.

7. Place your left foot stamper on the sidewalk and press down all around to make a nice, clean footprint. Carefully remove by using the handle.

8. Move down the sidewalk a nice giant's step worth. Now use the right foot stamper. Repeat, alternating feet, until you run out of paint or get hungry and thirsty.

9. Spread the story about the strange news report that you read (aliens, dinosaurs, Bigfoot, giant invaders—escaped in the city!) Make up your own newspaper story (see previous page) to hand out to your family and neighbors to explain the mysterious footprints.

slapstick
Story Time

Get ready to laugh with this fun-by-numbers game. On your paper, write the numbers 1 to 16 down the left side of your page. Ask your friend to supply the key words and record them on your paper. Then read out the adventure story at right, filling in the words your friend supplied that correspond to the numbers in brackets.

YOU'LL NEED
a friend
paper
pencil

YOU WILL NEED THESE KEY WORDS IN THIS ORDER:

1. person's name
2. place
3. thing
4. another thing
5. another person's name
6. adjective (a word that describes something, e.g. pretty, purple, sleepy)
7. another adjective
8. kind of animal
9. adverb (a word that describes an action, e.g. happily, crazily, slowly)
10. still another adjective
11. kind of feeling (e.g. sad, scared, excited)
12. part of your body
13. verb (an action word, e.g. run, dance, play)
14. another verb
15. one more verb (past tense—ends in -ed)
16. another adverb

Once up on a time, **(1)** was taking a walk in **(2)** when (s)he was tapped on the shoulder by a **(3)**.

"Excuse me," said the **(3)**, "but you have a **(4)** in your hair. May I remove it?"

"No," said **(1)**, "I am on my way to meet **(5)** and I want him/her to think I look **(6)**."

The **(3)** flew away and **(1)** continued on the journey. Soon (s)he came to a **(7)** cottage in the woods. It looked like it belonged to a **(8)**. **(1)** knocked on the door. The door opened **(9)**. **(5)** came to the door.

"Hello, **(5)**," said **(1)**. "You look very **(10)** today. Are you feeling **(11)**?"

"Well, I just had my **(12)** removed. It makes me feel like I want to **(13)** and **(14)**. Would you like to do that together?"

So **(1)** and **(5)** **(15)** off together into the distance. And they lived **(16)** ever after.

Tip-Toe Tommy Toad

Meet Tip-Toe Tommy Toad, the fastest toad in the west. You can make your own leaping critter using the traditional Japanese paper-folding art called origami. Make a few toads with your friends for a jumping contest or a hopping race to a finish line.

HERE'S WHAT TO DO: Origami begins with a perfectly square piece of paper. Origami paper works best, and can be found at any art supply, craft, or toy store. Regular bond paper will work too, but must be made into a perfect square. Fold as follows to make your toad:

1 Fold the square in half.

2 Fold top edge down to meet bottom edge to create fold **A**. Unfold. Fold top edge down to fold **A** to create fold **B**. Unfold.

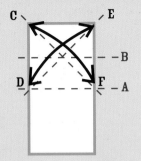

3 Fold point **C** until it touches point **F**. Unfold. Fold point **E** until it touches point **D**. Unfold. Fold horizontally along fold **B** so **C** touches **D** and **E** touches **F**.

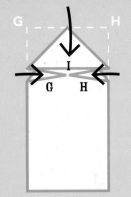

4 Push the top corners **G** and **H** inward to meet at point **I**. Flatten. The paper should now look like a house. This is the toad's head.

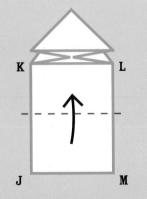

5 Fold the bottom edge up so that point **J** touches **K** and point **M** touches point **L**.

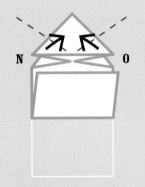

6 Fold points **N** and **0** up to stick out past the edge of the head like ears. Flatten.

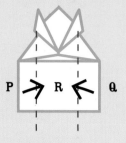

7 Fold sides **P** and **Q** along the dotted lines towards point **R** in the center. Let the paper nestle below the "ears." Do not fold the "ears."

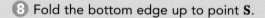
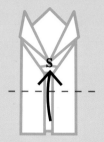

8 Fold the bottom edge up to point **S**.

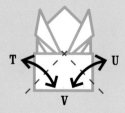

9 Fold corners **T** and **U** down to point **V**, then unfold.

10 Pull points **W** and **X** out from behind the front flap and flatten. The shape should now look like the bottom of a boat.

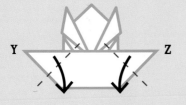

11 Fold points **Y** and **Z** down to form the toad's legs.

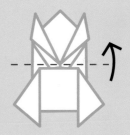

12 Fold the toad in half so that the bottom feet reach the front feet.

13 Finish by folding the piece with the back legs in half in the opposite direction.

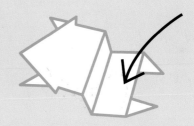

14 Press on the toad's tailbone to make it jump. How well and how far it will jump will depend on how neat your folds are. A little practice will make your toadie really hop!

What did the toad order at the fast food restaurant?

French flies and a diet Croak.

What do fashionable toads wear when relaxing at the pond?

Jumpsuits.

What kind of shoes do frogs wear?

Open-toad.

"Waiter, waiter... do you have frog legs tonight?"

"No, indeed...! I always walk this way."

Why did the frog croak?

Because it ate a poisonous fly.

Why are frogs so happy?

They eat whatever bugs them.

What do you call a frog eye doctor?

A hoptometrist.

Hopping Humor

Why did the toad go to the hospital?

It needed a hopperation!

What does a frog wear on St. Patrick's Day?

Nothing!

What did the toad dress up as on Halloween?

A prince.

Ribbit!

What do you call it when a toad sees a mirage?

A hoptical illusion.

What's green, green, green, green, green?

A frog rolling down a hill.

How many frogs does it take to screw in a lightbulb?

One frog and 37 lightbulbs. Slippery hands, you know.

How FUNNY Are You?

Are you the life of the party? Or are you about as funny as a three-day math test?

Take the following quiz, writing your answers on a piece of paper. When you're all done, add up your score using the chart on the right.

1 Choose the best punchline for: What's black and white and red (read) all over?

a) Skunk with sunburn
b) Zebra with sunburn
c) A newspaper

2 Which is the funniest thing you can wear to school?

a) A skunk on your head
b) Shorts on your head
c) Shoes

3 How many knock knock jokes are actually funny?

a) All of them
b) None of them
c) What's a knock knock joke?

4 Why did the psychic chicken cross the road?

a) To get to the "other side."
b) She read the farmer's mind, and it wasn't pretty.
c) She had predicted that the sky was going to fall on this side of the road.

10-20
BEANCOUNTER
Your favorite comedian is your math teacher and your funniest moment was the time you actually forgot to bring your pocket protector to school!

LESS THAN 10
SERIOUSLY UN-FUNNY
You should consider a career as a sleep therapist. Your jokes can cure anyone's sleepless nights.

5 Choose the funniest object:

   a) Whoopee cushion
   b) Snake in a can
   c) Truly enjoyable homework

6 Which is the funniest?

   a) Squeezing ten clowns into a car
   b) Squeezing ten teachers into a car
   c) Squeezing ten basketballs into your bookbag

7 Which is the funniest?

   a) Guava juice
   b) Fried camel boogers
   c) Your baby brother's attempt to eat spaghetti

8 When you tell a joke, your friends usually:

   a) Laugh like maniacs
   b) Roll their eyes
   c) Friends? What friends?

9 People often describe you as:

   a) Pretty funny
   b) Class clown
   c) Zzzzzz...

10 Which animal is the funniest?

   a) A piranha with a toothache
   b) A giraffe with a stiff neck
   c) An elephant with a stuffy nose

SCORING

For each answer, give yourself the following points:

1	a: 3	b: 2	c: 5
2	a: 5	b: 3	c: 2
3	a: 5	b: 3	c: 2
4	a: 5	b: 3	c: 2
5	a: 5	b: 3	c: 2
6	a: 2	b: 3	c: 5
7	a: 2	b: 3	c: 5
8	a: 5	b: 3	c: 2
9	a: 3	b: 5	c: 2
10	a: 3	b: 2	c: 5

Add up your total and check against the laff-o-meter for your score.

21-29
FUNSTER

Okay, so you're not the class clown, but your mother thinks you're really funny. You like a good laugh, but you also have a serious side.

30-39
RULER OF REVELRY

Your witty wisecracks bring sunshine to the gloomiest of days. You're the official "cheer-er upper." You even make yourself laugh.

40-50
LAFF RIOT

You have a future in stand-up comedy, so don't sit down! You are so funny your friends need to spend time away from you to catch a breath.

Laff-O-Meter

Super Statuette of Your

figurines are nice to have, especially if they are trophies from winning the big championship game. Wouldn't you love to have a memento of your very favorite person, your real idol, your...Self!

1. Study your photo. Aren't you gorgeous? Kiss picture a few times.

2. Cut your image out of the picture. Be careful not to amputate any bits of your precious body when you are snipping.

3. Kiss picture again. Then glue your picture onto the cardboard. Allow it to dry.

4. Carefully cut around the edges of your photo through the cardboard.

5. Leave a space below the feet, about 1 cm ($1/2$ in.), to attach the base. Cut the bottom straight across.

6. Glue three popsicle sticks on top of each other into two stacks of three.

7. Glue the stacks on their sides to the front and back of the cardboard (see illustration). Allow to dry. Your finished statuette should stand on its own.

8. Use your markers to decorate the base of the trophy, include your achievement or special title.

9. Kiss. Display.

Magnificence

YOU'LL NEED

full-length photo of yourself

scissors

thick cardboard as big
as your picture

white glue

6 popsicle sticks

markers

superstar

57

Bread Bag Tag Racers

Make your own personal watercraft, following the steps at right, using those little square thingies used to tie up a bag of bread. Then race your boat against a friend's for some good clean fun.

TRACING TEMPLATE

YOU'LL NEED

tracing paper

pencil

scissors

index cards 7.5 x 13 cm (3 x 5 in.)

tape

waterproof markers

square plastic bread bag tags

superglue or rubber cement

water

large dishpan, bathtub, or kiddie pool

dishwashing soap

*Why do you have to refill the water container after each race? The answer is "Surface Tension." No, the boats are not tense and nervous. The tiny water molecules are.

In a container of water, all the molecules pull and grab each other. The water molecules at the top are only pulled on from below, forming a kind of "skin" at the surface. This skin is known as surface tension.

1 Lay the tracing paper over the boat template at left and trace around dotted line with pencil.

2 Carefully cut the boat out of the tracing paper.

3 Lay the tracing paper onto your index card. You might want to use small pieces of tape to hold it in place.

4 Using your pencil, carefully draw around the outline of the boat onto the index card. Cut out.

5 Decorate with water-proof markers.

6 Attach the bread bag tag to the back of your boat using superglue or rubber cement. The hole in the tag is your "engine."

Make sure the hole is hanging off the back of the boat.

7 Fill your container with about 2 cm (1 in.) of water.

8 Arrange your boats in a line. Drop a bit of dish-washing soap into the hole of each bread bag tag, and the race begins! Your boats will zoom off.

9 After each race, you'll have to empty out all the water and refill your container*, so keep the amount of water you use to a minimum.

VROOM BOAT

Adding soap to the boat's rear "engine" causes the water molecules back there to stop pulling on each other. Meanwhile, at the front of the boat, the surface tension is still strong. The grabby little water molecules at the front pull the boat forward. V-v-vroom! Once the soap gets spread around, the surface tension is broken, and a new boat won't get pulled. You will have to empty your pan, rinse out any soap residue, and start over with soap-free water.

You will make your own fortune cookies.

yummy things
to
Make and Eat

Treats ar

Truffle UFOs

Gross-Out Gummi Worms

Marzipan Moonsters

You will be glad you turned the page.

...n your future.

Fortune Cookies

Plutonian Pretzels

Gross-Out
Gummi Worms

YIELD: makes 48
PREP. TIME: 20 minutes

YOU'LL NEED

395 mL (1 2/3 cup) grape juice

395 mL (1 2/3 cup) fruit punch

2 packets unflavored gelatin, 15 mL (1 tbsp.) each

YOU'LL ALSO NEED

measuring cup

2 medium pots

2 rectangular pans 23 x 30 cm (9 x 12 in.)

oven mitts

mixing spoon

24 jumbo drinking straws cut in half

cutting board

rolling pin

1 Pour the different juices into separate pots, and bring to a boil. Ask an adult to help you with this step, and step 3.

Warning! As hot as lava!

2 Pour one packet of gelatin into each rectangular pan.

3 Put on oven mitts. Pour the hot grape juice into one pan. Pour the hot fruit punch into the other pan.

4 Stir both until the gelatin is completely dissolved.

5 Lay straws lengthwise in the pans. You'll want to submerge them so that the straws fill with the juice mixture. Use a spoon to push them down—but don't squish them!—the liquid will be very hot. If they float to the surface, put an empty jar on top to hold them down.

6 Refrigerate the pans with the straws in them until the gelatin is set, at least 3 hours (overnight is best).

7 When your gelatin is set, you are ready to remove your gummi worms from the straws. Lay the straws on a cutting board.

8 Gently roll and push the rolling pin along the straws so the gummi worms squish out the other end (see illustration).

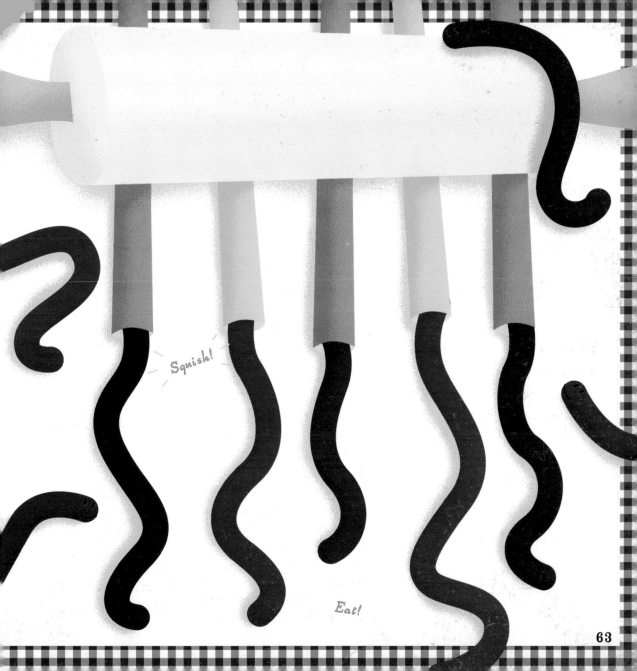

Squish!

Eat!

63

Wriggling Humor

What do you call a worm that's edible?

A yummi worm!

What did the worm say to the mole?

I guess we're on the ground floor.

Knock, knock.
Who's there?
Worm.
Worm who?
Worm in here, isn't it?

What do you call twelve inch-worms?

A foot.

What do you get if you cross a worm with an elephant?

Big holes in your garden.

Why did the worm cross the playground?

To get to the other slide.

What is the best advice to give a worm?
Sleep late.

What happens when you cross a bird and a worm?
Lunch time!

Why did the worm go to the library?
It was a bookworm.

What did the mother earthworm say when the teenage earthworm was late for dinner?
Where on earth have you been?

How much did the worm pay for its house?
Hardly anything, it was dirt cheap.

How do you find out which end of a worm is its head?
Tickle it in the middle and see where it smiles!

SUPER candy factory

These "out-of-this-world" recipes will make your day super-sweet, even if you have to share with your extraterrestrial controllers, er, parents. Some of these recipes will require help from an adult: be extra nice the day you decide to ask for help.

YIELD: makes 20
PREP. TIME: 15 minutes

Automatic Chocolate Stirring Devices

YOU'LL NEED

250 mL (1 cup) chocolate chips

YOU'LL ALSO NEED

measuring cup

microwavable bowl or double boiler

20 plastic spoons

waxed paper

ribbon

1 Melt chocolate chips in a double boiler or the microwave. You should ask an adult or extraterrestrial with opposable thumbs for help with this step.

2 Carefully dip each spoon into the melted chocolate, covering the spoon with the mixture. Leave 2.5 cm (1 in.) at the top of the handle.

3 Place the coated spoons on the waxed paper to cool and harden. For faster results, put the spoons in the fridge.

4 When the chocolate spoons are set, tie each handle with a ribbon. Use to stir hot chocolate for an extra delicious treat.

Marzipan Moonsters

YOU'LL NEED

500 g (1 lb) marzipan*
(almond paste)

food coloring

gumdrops in various colors

YIELD: makes 12
PREP. TIME: 30 minutes

YOU'LL ALSO NEED

4 medium bowls

toothpicks

cookie sheet

1. Knead the marzipan with your ten hand projections (fingers, in earthspeak) until it is soft enough to work with. About 30 seconds.

2. Divide your "dough" into quarters and place each into a separate bowl. Add a few drops of blue food coloring to one part; add a few drops of yellow to the second part; red to the third; and green to the last. Knead each dough ball again to spread the color evenly throughout each one. If you prefer a streaky look, mix the dough less evenly.

3. Roll a ball of any color about the size of a golf ball. This is your Moonster body.

4. Roll a smaller ball. This is your Moonster head. Stick it onto your Moonster body. Smooth together and shape your Moonster.

5. Use gumdrops to add details such as red eyes, yellow horns, a tail—it's up to your imagination. Use the toothpicks to carve fine details into your Moonsters.

6. As you finish making them, place each Moonster on a cookie sheet.

*WARNING: Do not use this recipe if you have a nut allergy.

alien
candy factory II

YOU'LL NEED

500 mL (2 cups)
chocolate chips
125 mL (1/2 cup)
peanut butter*

YOU'LL ALSO NEED

measuring cups
microwavable bowl
or double boiler
mixing spoon
teaspoon
cookie sheet lined
with waxed paper

Saturn Swirls

YIELD: makes 24
PREP. TIME: 25 minutes

1 Melt chocolate chips in a double boiler or in the microwave. You should ask an adult for help with this step.

2 Measure peanut butter and swirl into melted chocolate with mixing spoon. Do not mix completely—you should be able to see the two different color swirls.

3 Use the teaspoon to drop globs of the choco-peanut mixture onto cookie sheet lined with waxed paper.

4 Freeze until they reach the atmospheric temperature of Saturn or until solid, whichever comes first.

*ALTERNATIVE:
If you have a nut allergy, substitute white chocolate or butterscotch chips for the peanut butter.

Martianmallows

YOU'LL NEED

250 mL (1 cup)
boiling water

2 packets
unflavored gelatin,
15 mL (1 tbsp.) each

250 mL (1cup) sugar

5 mL (1 tsp.) vanilla

125 mL (1/2 cup)
icing sugar

YOU'LL ALSO NEED

mixing bowl

egg beater, whisk,
or electric mixer

23 x 36 cm (9 x 14 in.)
baking pan lined with
greased waxed paper

spatula

butter knife

plate

1 In a mixing bowl, dissolve the gelatin in the boiling water. You should ask an adult for help with this step.

2 Add sugar and vanilla.

3 Whip the mixture until it begins to look like creamy marshmallow fluff. This will take up to 20 minutes with an egg beater; longer with a whisk; 15 minutes with an electric mixer.

4 *Do Not Underbeat.* You need to trap enough air in your mixture to make it really marshmallowy.

5 Place the greased waxed paper in the baking pan. Spread the mixture on top evenly with a spatula.

6 Cover with waxed paper and allow the Martianmallow to sit overnight at room temperature.

7 Cut the Martianmallow into small cubes with the butter knife.

8 Roll each cube in icing sugar on a plate. Float them in hot chocolate or eat as is!

YIELD:
makes 100

PREP. TIME:
30 minutes

69

It's a Fact!

Dazzle your family and friends with these funky, freaky, fascinating, fantastic facts.

EXCUSE YOURSELF, ELSIE
The average cow burps 280 L (74 gal.) of gas every day!

LYIN' DOWN ON THE JOB
Most lions prefer sleeping on their backs. (This sounds better than lions that prefer to sleep on our backs!)

TALK ABOUT FLUFFY TOWELS
Starlings, a type of bird, are known to dry themselves off after a bath by rubbing themselves on sheep.

WATCH WHERE YOU'RE WALKING
Butterflies taste with their feet.

LEAVE A MESSAGE WITH MY ASSISTANT
Some Japanese cows have been fitted with pagers so they can be "beeped" when it's time to come in to the barn to be milked.

SAD BUT TRUE

Some scientists believe that the only animal other than us that cries when it's upset is the elephant. Good thing it doesn't also stamp its feet.

BECAUSE IT'S HARD TO DO STANDING UP

Giraffes sleep only three hours a night.

NO, YOU GO FIRST

The first earthling in space was a Russian dog named Laika.

WATCH OUT, OR YOUR FACE WILL STAY LIKE THAT

Crocodiles can't stick their tongues out.

CAN YOU PRESS PENTHOUSE, WITH YOUR BEAK?

The Peabody Hotel in Memphis, Tennessee, has some celebrity guests: five ducks that live on the roof, but take the elevator down every day to bathe in the lobby fountain.

ALIEN
candy factory III

Chocolate Space Spiders

YIELD: makes 24
PREP. TIME: 15 minutes

YOU'LL NEED

170 g (6 oz.) semi-sweet chocolate (6 squares)

250 mL (1 cup) butterscotch chips

250 mL (1 cup) mini marshmallows

250 mL (1 cup) peanuts* (optional)

500 mL (2 cups) crunchy chow mein-style noodles

YOU'LL ALSO NEED

measuring cups

microwavable bowl or double boiler

mixing bowl

mixing spoon

teaspoon

cookie sheet lined with waxed paper

1. Melt the chocolate and butterscotch chips together in the microwave or double boiler. Stir. You should ask an adult for help with this step.

2. Remove from heat. Add marshmallows, peanuts, and noodles. Stir lightly, being careful not to break the noodles—these will be the spiders' legs.

3. Using a teaspoon, drop the mixture onto a cookie sheet lined with waxed paper. Let cool for 30 minutes in the refrigerator. Do not release in vicinity of spaceships.

*ALTERNATIVE: *If you have a nut allergy*, you can substitute 250 mL (1 cup) raisins for the peanuts.

Plutonian Pretzels

YOU'LL NEED

8 g (2 1/4 tsp.) envelope
instant yeast
375 mL (1 1/2 cups) warm water
15 mL (1 tbsp.) sugar
15 mL (1 tbsp.) salt
1 L (4 cups) flour
1 egg
Kosher salt (optional)

YOU'LL ALSO NEED

measuring cups & spoons
large mixing bowl
mixing spoon
cookie sheet
small mixing bowl
egg beater or fork
pastry brush
oven mitts

Preheat oven to 220°C (425°F). Ask an adult for help with this step.

1. In a large mixing bowl, combine yeast, water, sugar, and salt.

2. Stir in the flour. Knead mixture with your clean hands on a clean work surface until the dough is smooth. About 5 minutes.

3. Pinch off lumps of dough about the size of a walnut. Model the lumps of dough into horrible monsters or wacky aliens. Add extra bits of dough as needed to sculpt. Keep in mind that your pretzels will expand and rise into crazy shapes in the oven, so don't worry about too much detail.

4. Place finished critters on an ungreased cookie sheet.

5. Crack egg in a small bowl and beat with an egg beater or fork until yolk and egg white are mixed. Using a pastry brush, lightly dab Plutonians with the beaten egg.

6. Sprinkle a little Kosher salt on each critter if you like your snacks salty.

7. Bake for 15 minutes at 220°C (425°F), or until brown on top. Use oven mitts to remove. Turn off oven, and allow to cool.

YIELD:
makes 30

PREP. TIME:
25 minutes

SLAPSTICK STORY TIME

YOU'LL NEED
a friend
paper
pencil

Here's a hilarious game you can play to pass the time while you wait for your delicious kitchen creations to bake, chill, or set. Turn to page 46 for directions, then prepare for the laughs.

YOU WILL NEED THESE KEY WORDS IN THIS ORDER:

1. thing
2. person
3. texture (e.g. furry, rough, slimy)
4. color
5. shape
6. something your mother likes to say
7. verb (action)
8. body part
9. another verb
10. another verb
11. another verb
12. another thing
13. feeling
14. one more verb
15. place
16. another thing

Once upon a time, a very large (1)
fell out of the sky and landed on
(2)'s head. It was (3), (4), and (5).

(2) screamed, "(6)!" then started to (7).

"Don't do that!" said the (1). "It hurts
my (8). If you keep that up, I will
have to (9)."

"Go right ahead!" said (2), starting to (10).

The (1) jumped up and began to (11).
It looked like a big (12). (2) felt very
(13) and started to (14).

Then the (1) flew off to (15) and was
never seen again. From that time on,
(2) had a strange mark on his/her
forehead that looked just like a (16).

ALIEN
candy factory IV

YOU'LL NEED

250 mL (1 cup) light corn syrup
175 mL (3/4 cup) margarine
250 mL (1 cup) peanut butter*
food coloring (2 colors)
750 mL (3 cups) flour

YOU'LL ALSO NEED

measuring cups
large mixing bowl
2 medium mixing bowls
mixing spoon
cookie sheet

Asteroidough

1. In a large mixing bowl, combine the corn syrup, margarine, and peanut butter into a dough-like consistency.

2. Divide the dough in half. Put one lump in one medium bowl, and one lump in the other bowl.

3. Add a different color of food coloring to each half, two drops is good to start. Blend with a spoon until the color in each bowl is even.

4. Add 375 mL (1 1/2 cups) flour to each bowl.

5. Blend flour into the dough with the mixing spoon. Then knead with your clean hands until the dough is smooth. If it seems sticky, add a little bit more flour. The dough should feel smooth and not stick to your fingers when you mold it.

6. Pinch off chunks and roll dough into little asteroids, each about the size of a golf ball.

7. Put the balls on a cookie sheet. Refrigerate asteroids overnight.

8. The next day, you can model the asteroidough into delectable aliens you can eat!

YIELD:
makes 24

PREP. TIME:
40 minutes

*WARNING: Do not use this recipe if you have a nut allergy.

YOU'LL NEED

80 mL (1/3 cup) unsalted nuts*
125 mL (1/2 cup) raisins
60 mL (1/4 cup) butter
80 mL (1/3 cup) shredded coconut

YOU'LL ALSO NEED

measuring cups
blender or food processor
spatula
small mixing bowl
fork
saucepan or microwavable bowl
teaspoon
small plate

*ALTERNATIVE:
If you have a nut allergy substitute the nuts with rolled oats.

Rocket Raisin Balls

1. Measure out nuts and chop in blender or food processor. (If you're using oats instead, they can be used directly from the bag.) Ask an adult to help with steps using the blender or food processor.

2. Remove chopped nuts with a spatula and place in a mixing bowl.

3. Measure out raisins into the blender or food processor and puree.

4. Remove pureed raisins with a spatula and add to nuts in mixing bowl. Using the fork, mix together well.

5. Melt butter in the microwave or on the stove, with adult supervision.

6. Add the butter to raisin-nut mixture and stir together well with fork.

7. Measure out the coconut onto the plate. Take a teaspoon-sized portion of the raisin mixture and roll it into a small ball in your clean hands.

8. Drop balls onto plate and roll to coat with coconut.

9. Refrigerate until they set (one hour).

YIELD: makes 20
PREP. TIME: 20 minutes

ALIEN
candy factory V

YOU'LL NEED
80 mL (1/3 cup) chocolate chips

125 mL (1/2 cup) butter

30 mL (2 tbsp.) heavy (whipping) cream

30 mL (2 tbsp.) icing sugar

cocoa powder

chocolate sprinkles

YOU'LL ALSO NEED
measuring cups & spoons

microwavable bowl or double boiler

mixing spoon

mixing bowl

2 plates

teaspoon

food container with lid

Truffle UFOs

YIELD: makes 24
PREP. TIME: 15 minutes

1. Melt the chocolate chips and butter together in the microwave or double boiler. You should ask an adult for help with this step. Remove from heat.

2. Add the cream. Stir.

3. With the mixing spoon, gradually stir in the icing sugar. Watch for lumps and smush them.

4. Let the mixture stand in a covered bowl, in a cool, dry place, overnight. Do not cool in the refrigerator.

5. Pour some cocoa onto a plate. Pour some chocolate sprinkles onto another plate.

6. Take about a teaspoon of the mixture and roll in your clean hands to form a small ball. Roll each ball to coat in either the cocoa or the sprinkles.

7. Store the finished UFOs in a covered container in the fridge. Remove from the fridge about 1 hour before eating.

YOU'LL NEED

20 mL (1 1/2 tbsp.) butter

375 mL (1 1/2 cups) brown sugar

90 mL (6 tbsp.) water

1.5 kg (6 cups) popcorn or 1 bag light microwave popcorn

250 mL (1 cup) nuts* (optional)

YOU'LL ALSO NEED

measuring cups & spoons

saucepan with lid or microwavable bowl

mixing spoon

candy thermometer

wooden mixing spoon

large bowl

Interstellar Space Junk

1 Melt the butter in the microwave, or a saucepan on the stove. You should ask an adult for help with this step, and steps 2 and 3.

2 In a saucepan, add brown sugar and water to the melted butter. Mix well until all sugar is dissolved.

3 Over medium heat bring to a boil. Cover the saucepan and boil rapidly for 3 minutes, or until the steam has washed any crystals off the sides of the saucepan.

4 Uncover and cook on medium heat without stirring, until the mixture reaches 114°C (238° F) on a candy thermometer, about 1 minute longer.

5 In a large bowl, carefully pour the caramel syrup over the popped popcorn. Add the nuts to the mixture, if using. **Be careful**: the caramel is **hot**.

6 Use a wooden spoon to spread the caramel evenly on the nuts and popcorn. Cool until you can touch it with your fingertips, about 5 minutes. It should still be warm and malleable.

7 Moisten your fingers with butter or vegetable oil. Grab small handfuls of the popcorn mixture and shape into planets, spaceships, or any other shape you like.

YIELD: makes 1.5 kg (6 cups)

PREP. TIME: 20 minutes

*****WARNING:**
Do not use nuts if you have a nut allergy.

79

FORTUNE COOKIES

Prediction...you will have...something delicious to eat in the next few minutes! There's nothing better than telling the future over something yummy like these authentic Fortune Cookies. You are guaranteed to have a sweet moment. (Then again, you might have a "crumby" one.) Have an adult help you with the stove.

You can use the fortunes below for a laff-a-minute. Simply copy them onto strips of paper using a ballpoint pen (do not use a felt tip pen or computer printer—the ink will run and your cookies will get disgustingly inky!) Of course, you can also make up your own wacky fortunes.

YIELD:
makes 10

PREP. TIME:
20 minutes

Wisdom is... Legend. Learned.

You have a crumb on your upper lip.

You're a lucky star.

Don't smile when you read this.

Do not reveal your fortune.

Beware of fanged friends who ask you for dinner.

Do you feel fortunate?

Help! I am being held captive in a fortune cookie factory!

YOU'LL NEED

30 mL (2 tbsp.) sugar

15 mL (1 tbsp.) cornstarch

30 mL (2 tbsp.) vegetable oil

1 egg

60 mL (1/4 cup) cold water

YOU'LL ALSO NEED

10 strips of paper for the fortunes, each 7.5 cm (3 in.) long

ballpoint pen

measuring cups & spoons

mixing spoon

mixing bowl

small non-stick frying pan

spatula

fork

muffin pan

Before you begin baking, prepare your fortunes. Lay them out in a handy place near your work surface, but not next to the stove.

1 With a large spoon, mix sugar and cornstarch together in a bowl.

2 Add the oil, egg, and cold water. Mix until smooth.

3 Heat a small, non-stick frying pan over low heat. Ask an adult for help with this step.

4 Spoon 15 mL (1 tbsp.) of batter into the hot pan. Using the back of the spoon spread into a thin circle, about 7.5 cm (3 in.) across.

5 Cook for 4 minutes or until cookie has begun to set.

6 Using a spatula, flip the cookie over and cook for one more minute. The cookie should be slightly golden, with darker edges.

7 With the spatula, remove the cookie from the pan onto a clean surface. Immediately lay a fortune strip across the center of the cookie.

8 Fold the cookie in half ⊙ ◖. **Be careful**: the cookie will be **hot**, and you've got to fold them up before they cool and harden. You might want to use a fork to help you fold the cookies over.

9 Fold the cookie in half again, this time in the opposite direction ⊙ ◡.

10 Place the warm cookie, tips down, in a muffin tin to cool. It will set in the familiar fortune cookie shape.

You will travel to great places.

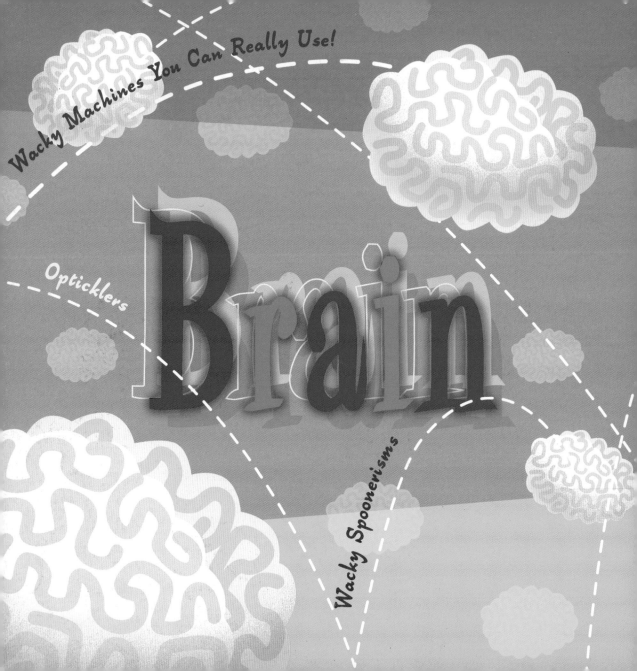

Wacky Machines You Can Really Use!

Opticklers

Brain

Wacky Spoonerisms

Pretzel Tongues

Napoleon's Code

Bogglers

Meet the Oddys

Opticklers

Can you fool your own brain? Take a look at these awesome optical illusions to find out!

Can you tell which edge of the picture frame is inside and which edge is outside?

Where's the missing slice of pie?

(Turn the book upside down.)

Bunny in a Hat

To put this rabbit into the magician's hat, look at the dot.
Then bring the page close to your nose.
The rabbit will jump into the hat. Now that's Magic!

Duck, duck...bunny?

(Turn the book 90° to the right to see this feathered friend's "fowl weather" personality.)

It's a Cat's Life

featuring "Rex"

It's a Fact!

More factual fuel to keep on astounding friends and family.

DOWN THE CHUTE
It takes food seven seconds to go from the mouth to the stomach via the esophagus.

TRY AGAIN, PROFESSOR
Albert Einstein's school principal thought he wasn't very smart and would never amount to anything.

GET OUT THE UMBRELLA, AND THE SHAMPOO
A raindrop can't form unless the air is dirty! Dust is needed for the moisture in a cloud to condense.

DROOL CITY
Every day, you produce enough saliva to fill about two cans of your fave soda.

THE "WATCH OUT FOR DOROTHY'S HOUSE NEXT TIME" WARNING
When you sneeze, the air whips from your mouth at 150 km (95 mi.) per hour—as fast as the winds in a cyclone or hurricane!

MY BABY'S A GENIUS
The average person learns half of everything he or she knows in the first five years of life.

GROSS MEDICAL FACTS
The first false teeth were made with teeth taken from dead bodies! Later types of dentures were made of wood, porcelain, or plastic.

THE "TOO MUCH INFORMATION" FACT
Only 30% of people in the world use toilet paper. The rest make do with leaves, rags, waste paper, and whatever else is available.

I'LL PASS ON THE PASTA
The world's record for the longest strand of spaghetti blown in a single blow out of a person's nose is 19 cm (7 1/2 in.) long.

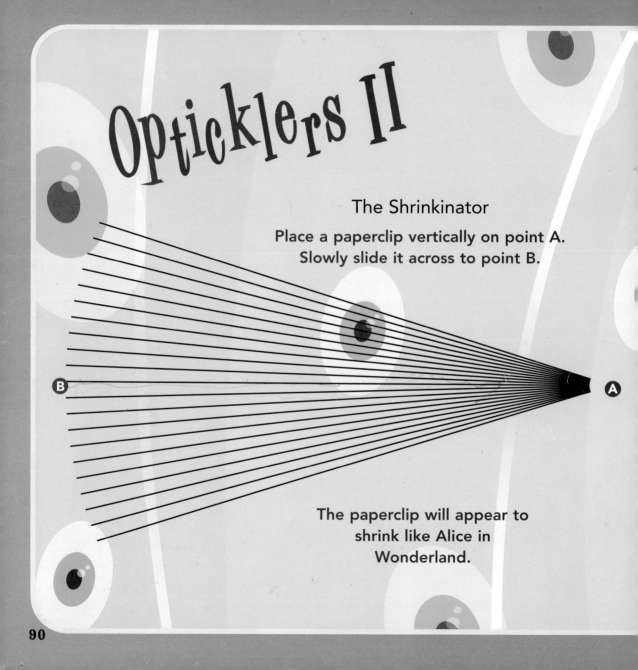

Opticklers II

The Shrinkinator

Place a paperclip vertically on point A.
Slowly slide it across to point B.

The paperclip will appear to
shrink like Alice in
Wonderland.

Bendo the Pencil

Place a pencil horizontally
across this design.
Is it suddenly crooked?

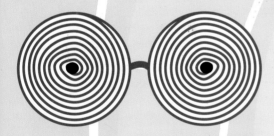

Look Deep Into My Eyes...

(Tip the book back and forth to
see these spooky eyes move!)

Magically Appearing Ghost

Stare at the ghost without moving
your eyes for 30 seconds. Quickly
look away, toward a white wall or a
blank piece of paper. Can you see
the ghoulish after-image?

Opticklers III

Secret Message

Embedded in the circular picture at right is a secret message. Can you read it? Tip the book away from you to a horizontal position. Next, bring the book up so it is level with your eye. Look straight across the image. You should be able to read word #1. Turn the book so that #2 is facing you and follow the same steps to read the second word of the magic message. Rotate the book to #3 and repeat. Did you get your three-word magic message?

Answer on page 160.

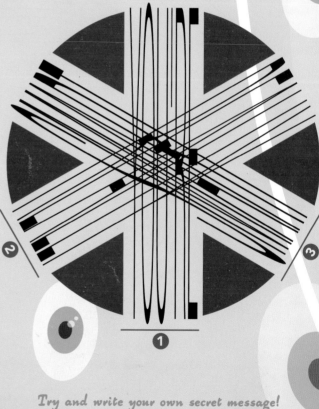

Try and write your own secret message!

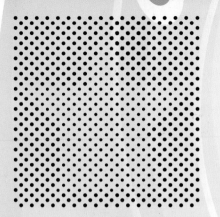

Can you see a picture
in the dot patterns?

**Move the picture side to side
to see a star appear!**

Happy or Sad?

**Turn the book upside down to
see an instant mood change.**

Open or Closed?

**Check out this woman's closed
eyes, and they will suddenly open!**

Pretzel Tongues

Six thick thistle sticks

Gig whip

Red leather, yellow leather

Greek grapes

Toy boat

A knapsack strap

Tiny orangutan tongues

Purple pimple liniment

Can you say these wacky word combos five times fast?

Billy's big blue badly bleeding blister

Rubber baby buggy bumpers

A box of biscuits, a box of mixed biscuits, and a big biscuit mixer

Slapped slimy slush shivers slightly

Three free throw pipes

Cross crossings cautiously

Robin redbreast's bad breath

Even Steven's even oven's on

THE Rubber Bandits
ARE YOU SAFE?
YOU NEVER KNOW WHAT DANGER LURKS ...INSIDE THE... KITCHEN JUNK DRAWER....
FREEZE!
PING!
PING!
PING!
HANDS BEHIND YOUR BACK OR WE'LL ATTACK!
OW!
SMACK!
TELL ME WHERE THE PENCIL STUBS ARE, AND QUICK!

Make sure this never happens to you!

Prevent attacks from rubber bandits with Rubberband Aids. The only device guaranteed to stop rubber bandits in their tracks.

97

WACKY MACHINES

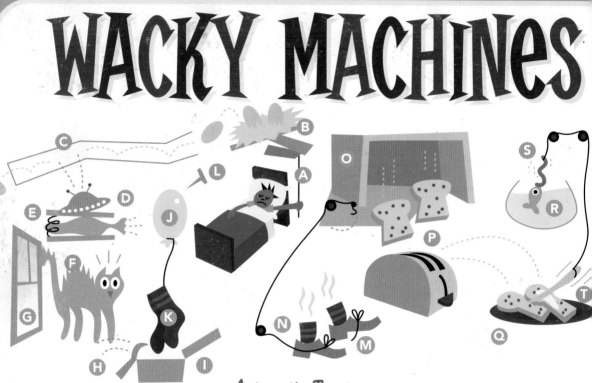

Automatic Toaster

Upon waking, hungry child pulls string (A), which runs up through chimney to platform under nest of loud, annoying blue jays. String pulls loose shingle, tipping nest (B), releasing eggs, which roll down, knocking loose alien spaceship (C) that has lodged within eavestrough. Spaceship plunges onto platform (D), which squeezes Whoopee cushion (E). Rude sound startles cat (F), which jumps through open window (G) into kitchen. Cat lands on ice cream scoop (H), which acts as lever to open box (I). Helium-filled balloon (J) carrying disgustingly ripe socks (K) rises out of box into air. Needle (L) pops balloon and socks fall into waiting pair of shoes (M), which start to walk away. Right shoelace (N) pulls open bottom of suspended box (O), allowing slices of raisin bread to drop into toaster (P). Finished raisin toast pops out of toaster and lands on plate (Q). Guppy in bowl (R) nibbles on fake worm (S), causing knife (T) to move back and forth, buttering toast perfectly.

You Can Really Use!

Automatic Milk-Pouring Machine

Upon waking, thirsty child pulls string (A), which turns on electric fan (B). Fan causes dog tickler (C) to revolve, causing Jack Russell terrier (D) to laugh so hard it chokes. Unconscious dog falls onto dog bed (E) next to gerbil cage, which causes hyper gerbil (F) to begin running for life. Rotating gerbil wheel pulls string tied to parrot's tail (G). Parrot flies into air, squawking, knocking into box containing 500 tennis balls (H). Gerbil wheel causes tennis racket (I) to repeat lousy serves until it hits tennis ball into target (J). Target releases grumpy principal (K) into icy-cold water tank (L). Water splashes out of tank and onto the street, where a passing foreign dignitary on an international peace mission (M) slips, careens along sidewalk and hits broom (N) propped up alongside porch. Broom tickles Jack Russell terrier (O). Dog jumps up tipping stand holding milk pitcher (P), and milk fills waiting glass.

more WACKY MACHINES

Automatic Toothpaste Squeezer

Rising sun (A) shines on magnifying glass (B), causing candle (C) to ignite. Rising smoke from candle makes ceiling fan (D) turn, resulting in refreshing breeze. Also pulls on string (E) attached to mother's hair iron (F), which clamps end of toothpaste tube (G). Toothpaste oozes onto toothbrush (H) held by hand of kid (I) who's very late for school.

Automatic Face Washer

Pigtailed sister's skateboard (A) pulls rip cord (B) setting wheels (C) in motion. Mother tries to feed mashed peas to howling baby in highchair (D). Baby sheds tears onto soapy washcloths (E), which (thwack, thwack, thwack!) scrub brother's face clean.

Bye, Mom!

Waaaah!

thwack
thwack
thwack!

You Can Really Use!

Automatic Dressing Machine

Older brother (A) falls to floor in mock surprise that sibling is experimenting with hygiene (see face-washing machine). Triggers secret lever in floor (B) that opens trapdoor. Freshly brushed and washed sibling (C) falls through hole into suspended T-shirt (D), clean underpants (E), and stinky soccer socks (F). Lands in kitchen where hungry, thirsty child retrieves waiting toast and milk… and goes to school without pants or shoes.

Ha ha ha hee hee ho ho ho!

click!

Ain't technology grand

munch munch

kooky calculator trix

Read the clues then type the numerical answer into your handy dandy calculator. Turn the calculator over to reveal the answer.

Answers on page 160.

1 What witches do at dinner time: **57337108**

2 What slimy creature took over New York? **8078**

3 Busy as a: **338**

4 What you wear in the science lab: **5376606**

5 Another word for alone: **.705**

6 Why you don't believe your sister: **5317345**

7 You put your foot in it: **3045**

8 What you want to be when you grow up: **5508**

9 Help! Help! **505**

10 Are you one of these, or do you keep your room neat? **8075**

11 Call the tooth fairy when one of your teeth is this: **35007**

12 What you yell to encourage a fish: **771606**

13 Is Mr. Claus in the room? **.40404**

14 What you yell when you meet a giant: **61834**

15 Snake's smooches: **535514**

16 French beauty: **37738**

17 What seven dwarves sing: **.4140414**

18 Sick island: **3751771**

Use the kookykode below to make up your own kooky calcuwords:

0=O

1=I

on/off

3=E

4=h

5=S

6=G

7=L

8=B

TRY THIS:

If you want to amaze your friends with your mathematical brilliance, have a pal type a secret three-digit number into the calculator. Ask them to multiply it by 7, then by 11, then by 13. Have them hand the calculator back to you. Press the = sign. The product will be a six-digit number. The first and last three digits will be the same as their secret number! Read out the three numbers and bask in their awe.

Wacky Word

Can you figure out what the next number, letter, or shape would be in each of the series below? **Answers on page 160.**

Example: O T T F F S S E N . . .

(Letters stand for **O**ne, **T**wo, **T**hree, **F**our, **F**ive, **S**ix, **S**even, **E**ight, **N**ine, so the next letter would be T for **T**en.)

① M ♡ 8 ♍ ☉ ❀ . . .

② ☽ ☽ ◐ ◯ ◑ ☾ . . .

③ QWERTY . . .

④ J F M A M J J . . .

⑤ a c e g i . . .

⑥ ½ 1 2 4 8 16 32 . . .

What do the following stand for?

Example: 12 M in a Y
(12 months in a year)

7 7 D in a W

8 52 C in a D

9 12 E in a D

10 5 F on a H

11 100 C in a D

12 2 W on a B

13 26 L in the A

14 365 D in a Y

15 360 D in a C

16 24 H in a D

17 60 S in a M

Series

Can you figure out the answers to these word puzzles?

Example:  = mixed-up kid

18 BAKED IDEA

19 Or Nothing
Or Nothing

20 Man
___
Board

21 Person   ality

22

23 Look
___
Out

24 Imageǝɓɐɯl

25 TTTT Winks

26 Wear
___
Stinky

27 My So There's a Fly up

28  CCCC

29 word
ord
d

30  o m
e
g
r
y   r

31 Somewhere
Rainbow

32 TWINS TWINS

33 READ
___

34 JOHNS

105

Gadzooks
Family Reunion

Meet the Gadzooks. They all have a striking family resemblance.

Not Gadzooks. They have been caught crashing the party.

Prunella

Happyjack

Eggsenham

Donald Frump

Canola Jane

Red

Nasty McNasty

Eric

Can you identify the rest of the party crashers? Answer on page 160.

Why did the bald man go outside?

To get some fresh hair.

with Detective Sherwack

Veronica Poopkin starring as *Bostonia Crème*

Scarlett Varlett as *"Dutchie"*

Sir Hugh Dunnit Noughtmie as *Ernst Kruller*

Elvin Clause as *Julio E. Glaziest*

Candy Kane as *Gimmea Duzzen*

Detective Sherwack and Doctor Wackson were attending the premiere of Agatha Twistie's new mystery, "Death by Donut." Just as the lights dimmed and the orchestra struck up, a scream filled the theater! Sherwack and Wackson rushed backstage where they found that the star, Veronica Poopkin, had been robbed of her diamond necklace. Sherwack and Wackson quickly apprehended the thief. These were their clues:

Elementary Fact #1: Veronica Poopkin's diamond necklace was kept in a heart-shaped box.

Elementary Fact #2: Veronica Poopkin's dressing room borders on the same number of dressing rooms as the thief's.

Elementary Fact #3: Veronica Poopkin's dressing room borders on the leading man's, Sir Hugh Dunnit Noughtmie.

Elementary Fact #4: Veronica Poopkin's dressing room also borders on that of Scarlett Varlett.

Elementary Fact #5: Candy Kane and Elvin Clause both have dressing rooms of the exact same size.

Elementary Fact #6: Because of an earlier tiff, Scarlett Varlett refused to use any dressing room that borders on Candy Kane's.

Who's the thief? Answer on page 160.

CAN YOU DECIPHER NAPOLEON'S CODE? **TURN THE PAGE TO FIND OUT HOW.**

Breaking the *Code*

Follow the steps below to figure out the secret code Napoleon is sending to his supporters.

1. On a piece of paper draw a graph with four horizontal **rows** (ie. four rows across) and five vertical **columns** (ie. five columns down), like this:

5 columns / 4 rows

2. Write each "word" (group of letters) from the message vertically in the grid, starting at the top left. Put the second "word" in the second column, the third "word" in the third column, and so on.

3. The letters from the message should completely fill your grid, like this:

T	H	E	B	I
E	E	H	C	G
S	E	I	S	C
G	N	I	M	O

The message can be read by starting at the top left corner and reading across the top **row**, then reading backwards along the second row, forwards again on the third row, and backwards on the last row. The message says, "The big cheese is coming."

You can use this trick to write and decipher your own secret codes. Using a pencil and paper, make a graph four rows across and five columns down. Write a twenty-letter message into the graph beginning at the top left, then going backwards across row two, alternating directions for each row.

Each **column** now contains your coded "words," the groups of four letters running down the graph. Write these on a slip of paper and pass to a friend.

For example, if your twenty-letter message was "Bring a video game for us," your graph would look like this:

B	R	I	N	G
E	D	I	V	A
O	G	A	M	E
S	U	R	O	F

And your code for your friend would be: **BEOS RDGU IIAR NVMO GAEF**.

Here's what your friend will have to do to decode your message:

1. Count the number of "words" (groups of letters) in the message. This is how many **columns** are needed. In this case, five.

2. Count the number of letters in each "word." This tells you how many **rows** are needed. In this case, four.

3. Draw a grid with this number of columns and rows.

4. From top to bottom, write each "word" in a **column** beginning at the left.

5. To read the message, start at the upper left corner. Read across the first row from left to right. Then read across the second row, from right to left.

6. Continue, alternating reading the rows from left to right, then right to left. The message will be revealed faster than a three-legged mare can get to Waterloo.

Lost Loot Line-Up

Check out the rogues' gallery below. One of the suspects is guilty of stealing Mrs. McGillicuddy's false teeth. Read the reports from the witnesses below to identify the Teeth Thief. All of the reports are accurate. Answer on page 160.

CLUES

1. Mrs. Tuna says the teeth thief had dark hair and a nose like a pig's snout.

2. Mrs. Bison is sure the thief was wearing glasses and a hat.

3. Mr. Turpentine said the perpetrator was bald and had a limp.

4. Mrs. Bagowind says the thief was dressed in shorts.

5. Little Junior Bagowind says the thief had on a blue suit and "walked funny."

SUSPECT 1
Sally Smith
Age: 94

Occupation:
Ski instructor

Can you say
"Teeth Thief"
ten times fast?

SUSPECT 2
Stan "the Man" Nitwit

Age: "Huh?"

Occupation:
Rope Jumper

SUSPECT 3
Rob A. Lotostuff

Age: 16

Occupation:
French Fryer

SUSPECT 4
Bill Toupé

Age: 18 going on 6

Occupation:
Wrestling turnips
into the pot

Wacky Spoonerisms

know your blows ✳ go and shake a tower ✳ stop nicking your pose

I'm shout of the hour ✳ **I hit my bunny phone**

eye ball ✳ lack of pies ✳ belly jeans ✳ fighting a liar

roaring pain

warty finks

Can you match these
"spoonerized" phrases
with what good ol' Arch
meant to say at right?

no tails

jinx and mules

my zips are lipped ✳ you have very mad banners

wave the sails ✳ lead of spite ✳ a blushing crow

bin and scones ✳ nosy little crook ✳ cattle ships and bruisers

I'm a damp stealer ✳ bite of the flumblebee

Reverend William Archibald Spooner was a professor at Oxford University, England, in the late 19th and early 20th centuries. He was famous for the wacky way he would mix up, transpose, and otherwise mangle his sentences.

But Spooner didn't "invent" spoonerisms. The Ancient Greeks had a word for spoonerisms of their own: metathesis, which means "the act of switching things around."

flight of the bumblebee ✳ pouring rain ✳ save the whales

✳ speed of light ✳ I'm a stamp dealer ✳

you have very bad manners ✳ jelly beans ✳ toe nails

go and take a shower ✳ **I hit my funny bone**

✳

✳ battle ships and cruisers ✳ cozy little nook

✳

blow your nose ✳ stop picking your nose ✳ I'm out of the shower

my lips are zipped ✳ lighting a fire

skin and bones ✳ bye all ✳ minks and jewels

pack of lies ✳ forty winks ✳ a crushing blow ✳

Slapstick Story Time

You can turn a familiar story into side-splitting good times. Turn to page 46 to find out how to make the hilarity happen.

YOU WILL NEED THESE KEY WORDS IN THIS ORDER:

1. animal
2. thing (e.g. shoe, apple, igloo)
3. objects (e.g. eggs, kittens, airplanes)
4. things that smell bad
5. strong material
6. person
7. adjective (a word that describes something, e.g. chunky, hot, smooth)
8. verb and verb (past tense—ends in -ed)
9. body part
10. thin object
11. another thing
12. kind of food
13. adverb (a word that describes an action, e.g. happily, slowly)

Once upon a time, there were three little (1)s that lived in a (2). The first little (1) built a house out of (3). The second little (1) built a house out of (4). The third little (1) built a house out of (5).

One day (6) came along and said, "I would like to blow down those (7) houses."

So (6) huffed and puffed and blew down the first house.

All the little (1)s ran to the house made of (4).

(6) huffed and puffed and blew down the second house.

All the little (1)s ran to the house made of (5).

(6) huffed and puffed. (6) (8). But (s)he could not blow down the third little house. So (6) climbed up on the (9) of the house and tried to slide down the (10).

Inside the house, the three little (1)s started a fire in the (11). (6) fell down into the fire and was cooked into a (12). The (1)s lived (13) ever after.

Animal
Ducktionary

If animals wrote the dictionary,
how different would our word definitions be?

apparent — King Kong's mom or dad

bear-headed — fur hat

boaring — a dull pig

cantelope — African deer that refuse to marry in secret

carp — nagging goldfish

catastrophe — feline crisis

crock — dangerous storage jar likely to bite off your hand

crowbar — telephone wire where single crows gather to meet

donkey — used to open donlocks

elephantasy — peanuts forever....

gazellevator — transportation device that goes from floor to floor in leaps and bounds

gerbilliards — snooker game played by talented rodents

gullible — foolish bird

hogwash — unusually tidy pig

lion-backer — roaring footballer

loonatic — crazy about birds

monkey wrench — tool for opening bananas

mousetache — upper lip décor with tail

offishal — finned football referee

orangutangle — apes wrestling

outraygeous — mantas with wild fashion sense

pandamonium — wild party (pandas with lampshades on their heads, etc.)

pants — out-of-breath insects

roostir — a spoon that says cock-a-doodle-doo

sealabration — wild party (seals with lampshades on their heads, etc.)

turtelevision — hard-shelled video device

viper — venemous tool for vashing vindows

Walk the plank, matie.

You first, Pinkster.

lady pink's
HIDDEN TREASURE

Lady Pink, the dreaded pirate of Capital Sea Playground, has buried her treasure somewhere in this park. Luckily you have found the map. Can you figure out the wacky directions and find the treasure? Don't be fooled by little tricks, the secret is buried somewhere in the colorful capital clues. **Answer on page 160.**

① batter's up! begin at home

② you hit it into foul (phew!) territory, sashay nine flip flops north— what a **D**ump

③ escape to the extreme southeast and don't h**I**de behind any rocks

④ six flip flops north— f**A**lse alar**M**—no point digging here

⑤ keep the sh**O**vel for a couple of scoops two flip flops **N**orthwest

⑥ head for the sha**D**e of a leafy tree

⑦ ay**E**, matie, our vessel **A**waits; nine flip flops no**R**thwest

⑧ treasure hunter over-board; st**R**ike **I**t rich in the light blue waters

⑨ **N**o fool's **G**old; take a few deep breath**S**, this is the spot!

= 1 flip flop step
(or a finger width)

N

W · E

S

Meet the Oddys

The Oddys is the strangest family you will ever meet. They eat snake feet for breakfast. They wash their hair once a year, whether it needs it or not. They love to talk, but hate to speak. Each of the Oddys has his or her own special quirks too.

Grandma Oddy loves to knit, but she never learned how to finish off, so for years she has been working on the same scarf. Grandma Oddy also has trouble keeping track of her letters when she writes. She *always begins a word with the wrong letter*.

Grandpa Oddy loves hip hop music and is a wonderful break dancer. Perhaps it's all those headspins that makes him *forget the first letter of every word he writes*.

Mama Oddy is a bus driver. She likes to drive her route backwards. She also *likes to put the wrong letter at the back end of all her words*, just to keep things hopping.

Papa Oddy is very good with animals. He trains turtles to play trumpet and tickles tarantulas. He *always puts his favorite letter—"t"—at the beginning of words*.

Martha Oddy is great at hockey and ping pong. She is terrible at spelling, because she *insists on leaving out the letter "s" when it appears in a word*.

Zack Oddy is a mixed-up kid. He'd rather sleep than play, clean than eat, and mow the lawn than climb a tree. He *always writes the wrong letter before the last letter in every word*.

Read the emails written by the Oddy family. Can you decide which Oddy wrote which sentence? Do you know what each email should actually say? **Answers on page 160.**

1 y avorite and s laying onight t he all.

2 Qy totalry cocl homewosk xs doge.

3 Nexe stot, Maix Streel Statiot!

4 Dould lou rike she fcarf ehen U'm fone?

5 If it' unny oon, we can go wimming.

6 Tould tou tike to tear tome tusic?

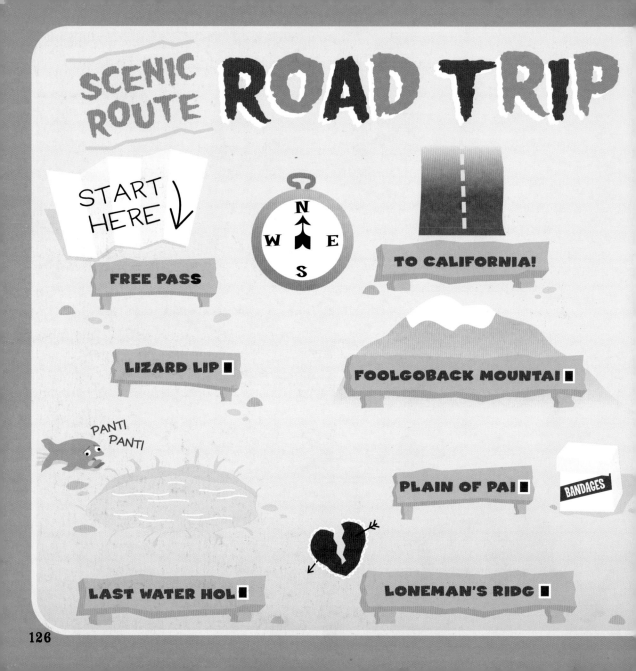

Each of the place names on the route map is missing its last letter. The last letter is either an N, S, W, or an E. Interestingly, these four letters each stand for directions— north, south, west, and east. Starting at Free Pass, can you follow the map by figuring out the last letter of each place name, then travel in that direction until you come to the next clue? Destination: California, and *no shortcuts!*

Check your answers on page 160.

WITCHES' BRE ■

TO OBLIVION, UTAH

ECHOING CAVER ■

COYOTE'S PA ■

ICY FINGER ■

GEORGE'S GORG ■

VALLEY OF NO RAI ■

Yolanda's POTION

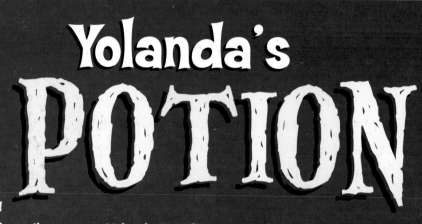

The evil sorceress Yolanda Bagobones is making a horrible potion that will turn children into monsters! But for some reason, her potion is not working. She is missing an important ingredient. Can you solve the word jumbles at right to discover what Yolanda is missing?

Are you missing an ingredient too—like how to do a Word Jumble Puzzle? Here's the recipe:

1. Beside each clue is a word jumble with one letter missing.
2. Grab a pencil and paper to copy each set of letters. Read each clue and rearrange the letters on your paper to spell out the answer, filling in the missing letter.
3. The missing letters are part of a final word jumble. When you've figured them out, write them down separately on your paper.
4. Unscramble the circled letters to make the seven-letter word that is Yolanda's mystery ingredient.

1. **Eyes of this animal are good for stew** W(E)T N = NEWT

2. **Used for flying** O R ◯ O M

3. **Male witch** C ◯ K W O R L

4. **Spirits** S H O ◯ T S

5. **Horrid** ◯ I R T R E L E

6. **Used for spells** G I M A C D ◯ W N

7. **Powerful word** A A B A B A ◯ R A D R

What is the missing ingredient? Answers on page 160.

Add the mystery ingredient to the recipe on the next page to make a totally awesome, disgustingly revolting magic brew of your own that really changes color! It's like, well, like magic!

YOU'LL NEED

approx. 1L (4 cups)
distilled water

1 whole red mystery ingredient

YOU'LL ALSO NEED

knife and cutting board

large saucepan with lid

large bowl

strainer

large wooden spoon

storage jar with lid

1. Chop up or shred the "mystery ingredient" (see page 128) into small pieces. Get an adult to help you with this step and steps 2 and 5. Place in a large saucepan.

2. Cover the "mystery ingredient" with distilled water. Bring to a boil.

3. Reduce heat. Cover and simmer for 20 minutes. Then let your potion cool for about 1 hour.

4. Place a large bowl in the kitchen sink. Pour the liquid from the saucepan through a strainer, and into the bowl. Press on the "mystery ingredient" with the wooden spoon to extract all of the juice.

5. Pour your potion into a storage jar. It is now ready for use.

Potion

RECIPE

To see the potion in action, you will need:

60 mL (1/4 cup) white vinegar

5 mL (1 tsp.) baking soda

60 mL (1/4 cup) tap water

spoonful baking soda

spoonful white vinegar

You will also need:

4 small containers
(small juice glasses are good)

1 Put 60 mL (1/4 cup) of vinegar in one container. Set aside.

2 Mix the baking soda with enough tap water to measure about 60 mL (1/4 cup). Put this mixture in a second container.

3 Keep some additional baking soda (a spoonful) handy in the third container, and some white vinegar in the last container for later use.

4 Gather your two victims, er, friends. Give one friend the container of white vinegar from step 1. Give the other friend the container holding the baking soda mixed with water from step 2.

5 Explain to your friends that you have cast a spell on each of them. Your spell will turn them into either a newt, or a bat. What color their witches' brew changes to will show them their fate. Pink or red means newt. Green means bat. Make sure you cackle dramatically at this point.

6 Take your potion (it should be a disgusting shade of blue) and very carefully, add some to friend #1's container. The liquid in your friend's container should turn pink or red. Aha! A newt!

7 Take your potion, and very carefully add some to friend #2's container. It should turn an icky green. Aha! A bat!

8 Tease your friends for a few minutes before offering to undo your spell.

9 To release the newt, add pinches of baking soda—about 1 mL (1/4 tsp.)—to his or her container until the pink liquid returns to its original color. It will make a very spooky fizzing and bubbling sound.

10 To release the bat, add dribbles of vinegar to his or her container until the green liquid returns to its original color.

Kangaroo Wrestling

Transformations

Games

Rooster Wrestling

You can rooster-wrestle with a large group of eight to twenty players. Run string along the ground to section off a large circle—about 3 m (10 ft.) across—to be the wrestling ring.

1. All the roosters should get into the circle. Try and leave space between yourself and the other roosters.

2. Squish down into a rooster position by grabbing an ankle with each hand.

3. Start hopping around the circle, toward your opponents. Make squawking rooster noises if you like.

4. The object of the game is to nudge your opponents out of the circle, *without letting go of your ankles*.

5. Players that are pushed out of the circle, or off balance, fall on their own, or let go of their ankles are out.

6. Watch out for "dominos," when one rooster knocks over a whole row of

Cock-a-doodle-doo!

other roosters! When this happens, all the knocked-over roosters must call out "Cock-a-doodle-doo!" Only the last rooster to crow is out; the others can remain in the game.

7 The last squatting rooster is declared the winner.

Boing!

Kangaroo

To play this hip-hop game, you just need two "kanga-wrestlers," some open space, and a sense of humor.

1. Clear a nice open space to be your wrestling ring. If some outback is not available, try a grassy area in a park or in the backyard. Do not attempt kanga-wrestling anywhere near Grandma's best china.

2. Face your opponent.

3. Grasp your opponent's left hand, as if you were about to shake hands.

4. Shake hands, since this would be the polite way to start a match.

Wrestling

5. Grab your right ankle with your right hand. You should both be standing on one foot.

6. On a count of three, using only your left hand, try to gently push and pull your opponent off balance.

7. The match is over when a player lets go of his/her ankle, lets go of the other player, or falls.

What's a kangaroo's favorite year?

A leap year.

Kangaroo Crack-Ups

Where do kangaroos go to the bathroom?

The kanga-loo!

How did the kangaroo get his car to run?

He jump-started it.

What did the kangaroo do when it ran out of food?

It went grocery hopping!

What do you call a lazy joey that doesn't go out to play?

A pouch potato.

Why did the kangaroo bring an extra pouch to the golf course?

Just in case it got a hole in one.

Why don't kangaroo mothers like rainy days?

Because the kids have to play inside.

How do you know if a kangaroo's upset?

It gets hopping mad.

What kind of hairstyles do joeys wear?

Kanga-dos.

What's a kangaroo's best basketball move?

The jump shot.

What did Sherlock Holmes say to Watson after solving the case of the missing kangaroo?

It was roo-dimentary, Watson!

Why was the mother kangaroo cross with her children?

Because they ate potato chips in her pouch and didn't vacuum.

WINDY INDY 500

Welcome, race fans, to the most exciting event on the racing circuit. The conditions on the track are fast, and the crowd is going wild, eager to see some non-stop action!

The Indy 500 is one of the oldest and most prestigious automobile races in the world. The race is held every year in Indianapolis, Indiana. The annual race is 805 km (500 mi.) long (hence the '500' in the name). Cars travel at speeds of approximately 355 km/h (220 m/h). YIKES—that's fast! Here's a home version.

YOU'LL NEED
sheets of white paper
colored markers
waxed paper
tape
drinking straws
food coloring
small cup
water

1. Draw a track on the paper. Use the picture here as a model. Add lots of fun obstacles, such as "Pile of homework!" or "Pit stop." Don't forget to include your start and finish lines.

2. When your track is complete, lay a sheet of waxed paper over it. You will still be able to see the track clearly through the waxed paper. Use some tape to secure it.

3. Mix a drop of food coloring into some water in a cup. Dip your straw in and make your car by tapping off a drop onto the "Start" line.

4. Put the straw in your mouth, and blow! Using only your own hot air, push the water blob along the track. Can you beat the clock, or your opponent's time? Be sure to stay on track.

141

Silent Movie Sound effects

a group of friends (best with eight or more people)

lots of interesting objects, try any of the items below, or find your own:

newspapers, paper bags, balloons, whistles, bells, rattles, pots, and spoons

When motion pictures were first invented in the late 1800s the movies were silent. So as soon as motion pictures came to a theater, so did sound effects. Sometimes a musician played or a whole troupe of actors traveled with the film, doing the voices and making the sounds of, say, horses or locomotives. Now it's a great party game.

1. Choose a few players to be the sound crew, a few to be the first actors, and the rest to be the audience. You can take turns and change the roles so everyone has a turn to be an actor and on the sound effect crew.

2. Take a few minutes to set the scene. Have the actors play out a scary moment, a comedy, or an action scene. Whatever you decide, remember that no sound must come from their lips!

3. The sound effects, of course, will come from the sound crew, who are ready to create a mixture of hilarious sounds using their props and their own shrieks, howls, hiccups, even words.

4. When the scene is over, and the audience stops laughing, have the actors become the sound crew, the audience members become the actors, and the sound crew becomes the audience.

BANG!

SCREEECH!

BOING!

CRASH!

Give a different scenario to the next group of actors, such as hysterical laughter, saying "I love you," or sobbing.

Bet you can't count to twenty—the Buzz, Fizz, Alleyoop way—without laughing. You can play this game anywhere, anytime.

YOU'LL NEED
a group of friends (three to ten people)

Buzz, Fizz

1 Begin with the number 1, and go around the circle, each person saying the next number.

2 The number 5 is BUZZ. Every time you say a number with a 5 in it, such as 15, or that is a multiple of 5, such as 10, you say BUZZ instead.

3 The number 7 is FIZZ. Every time you say a number with a 7 in it, such as 17, or that is a multiple of 7, such as 14, you say FIZZ.

4 The number 10 is ALLEYOOP. Every time you say 10, or a multiple of 10, make a whooping ALLEYOOP!

A SAMPLE COUNT TO TWENTY WOULD GO LIKE THIS:

1, 2, 3, 4, BUZZ, 6, FIZZ, 8, 9, BUZZ ALLEYOOP, 11, 12, 13, FIZZ, BUZZ, 16, FIZZ, 18, 19, BUZZ ALLEYOOP!

Players are "out" if they mess up the sequence, forget to say a FIZZ or a BUZZ, or if they get tongue-tied (saying something like FUZZ BIZZ is an *out*). The last player remaining wins the round.

Alleyoop!

To make sure the game goes at a snappy pace, if a player is taking too long, you can get them to hurry up by silently counting down from five. If the player has not yet moved on to the next number, they are out.

To make this game **easier**, leave out the FIZZ and ALLEYOOPS. Only say BUZZ for numbers that have a 5 in them, such as 15, but not the multiples.

To make the game **harder**, change the numbers you are using for FIZZ and BUZZ each round. You can also add another combination, such as SHEBANG for 3.

Will Fudgy Find A Way Out? Will the Mice Ever Return?
Will Fudgy Find a SUNFLOWER Seed? Stay Tuned for the Continuing Story of....
GERBIL JAILBREAK!!!!!!!

TRANSFORMATIONS

Can you transform a cat into a dog, or love into hate? You don't have to be a magician to make these quick changes, just play Transformations. You can play this word game by yourself, or in competition with a pal. The rules are easy. Try it out the next time you're on a long car trip and the next bathroom break is in the next state.

YOU'LL NEED

pencil and paper

1 Start with two words that have the same number of letters, like WORD and GAME. It's fun if the words are related. Three-letter words are good for beginners. Four-letter words offer a solid challenge.

2 The object of the game is to create the target word by changing only one letter at a time. Each change must make a real word.

CAT ➙ DOG ······ TOP ➙ HAT ······ GIVE ➙ TAKE

3 Here's one example of how to Transform WORD into GAME:

Change the D to an E	WORD > WORE
Change the W to a C	WORE > CORE
Change the O to an A	CORE > CARE
Change the R to an M	CARE > CAME
Change the C to a G	CAME > GAME

You have successfully changed WORD to GAME in five steps!

4 Once you've changed one letter to another, you can't reuse the previous letter again in that position. For example, if you change worD to worE, you can't use a D again for the fourth letter. (You can use it, though, in the other three places.)

5 There is frequently more than one way to transform the word. The *best* way would have the fewest number of steps.

6 Try your transformation powers on the word pairs along the bottom of the page. One possible solution for each is given on page 160.

7 Compare your solutions to a friend's. The shortest solution is the winning answer. If you're playing against yourself, see how many different solutions you can come up with for the same word combo.

READ → BOOK ⋯⋯⋯ FISH → HOOK ⋯⋯⋯ BOOK → WORM ⋯⋯ 149

STAR WARTS

Battle for the galaxy against the forces of evil! (If no evil forces are handy, you can compete against a friend.)

The object of the game is to get all of your warts onto all four points of your opponent's turf before your turf is invaded.

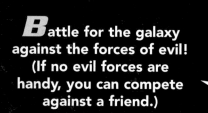

YOU'LL NEED

an opponent

4 pennies
(Empire warts)

4 dimes
(Rebel warts)

GAME RULES

1. Choose which player is "Empire" and which is "Rebel." Place your warts (coins) on the points in your turf.

2. The player with the longest fingernails goes first. The first move is always into the center.

3. Players now take turns moving one space at a time into a free space. You can move either into the center, or to an adjacent star point, provided there is no other wart on that spot. You cannot "jump" spaces.

4. If a player cannot move because the center and neighboring spots are blocked, he or she loses a turn.

5. A player wins when a complete turf invasion occurs—that is, when a player's warts are all on the other player's star points.

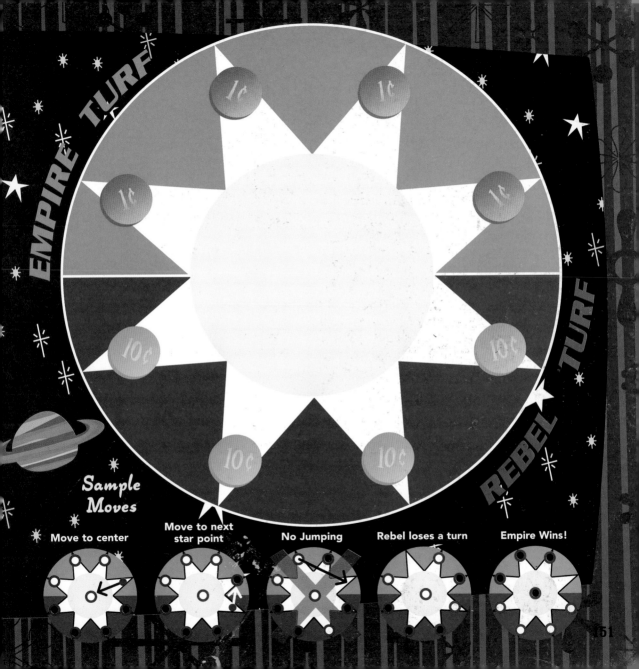

EMPIRE TURF

REBEL TURF

Sample Moves

Move to center

Move to next star point

No Jumping

Rebel loses a turn

Empire Wins!

151

It's a Fact!

The facts just keep on coming...

TRY ENFORCING THIS LAW
In North Carolina, it is against the law for dogs and cats to fight.

IT'S DR APPLE FARMER TO YOU
"Pomology" is the science of growing an apple.

ROYAL FACIAL HAIR
The king of hearts is the only king without a moustache on a standard playing card.

ONE CAN NEVER BE TOO POLITE
In England, in the 1880s, "pants" was considered a dirty word.

CAN YOU SPELL MISSISSIPPI BACKWARDS?
An earthquake on December 16, 1811 caused parts of the Mississippi River to flow backwards!

SICKLY SWEET

Chocolate was used as medicine during the 18th century. It was believed that chocolate could cure a stomachache.

USE THE BEST LINENS

Tablecloths were originally meant to serve as towels with which dinner guests could wipe their hands and faces after eating.

SMOG ALERT

Researchers have discovered that eating five or more apples a week is linked to better functioning of the lungs.

WONDER WHO MEASURED THIS TEMPERATURE

A lightning bolt generates temperatures five times hotter than those found at the sun's surface.

Sharks and Fish

**A high-stakes game of guessing and...more guessing.
Match wits with an opponent to see who can guess each
other's secret four-digit number in the shortest time.**

*It's all about being
in the right place at
the right time.*

YOU'LL NEED

an opponent
pencils
paper

1. Choose a four-digit number, such as 6478. You cannot use any of the same numerals twice (e.g. 3367 is not allowed).

2. Make a flap by tearing or folding a bit of paper over your number to hide it from your opponent, like this:

   6478

3. Your opponent does the same with his or her own secret number.

4. The player with the most buttons on his/her clothing goes first

5. Begin by trying to guess your opponent's number by saying a random four-digit number, such as 6798. Write this down so you can keep track of your guesses.

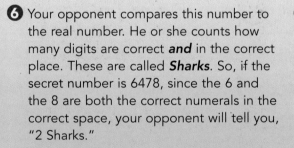

Easy for you to say. You've in the right spot, but I'm a little lost.

6 Your opponent compares this number to the real number. He or she counts how many digits are correct *and* in the correct place. These are called **Sharks**. So, if the secret number is 6478, since the 6 and the 8 are both the correct numerals in the correct space, your opponent will tell you, "2 Sharks."

7 Your opponent then looks to see how many numerals are correct, but are in the wrong spot. These are called **Fish**. In this case, the 7 is in the secret number, but it is in the wrong position. So your opponent says, "1 Fish."

8 Your turn is complete. Make sure you write down the score beside the number you guessed (6798—2 Sharks, 1 Fish). Most players would abbreviate this as 2S, 1F.

9 Now it is your opponent's turn to guess. Players take turns offering guesses and writing down the replies. You will have to use all your logic to figure out the answer from the clues your opponent gives you! See the next page for a sample game.

10 The first player that gets "4 Sharks"— all the correct digits in the correct positions—is the winner.

Sample Game:

1 First guess and results: **1234—1S, 2F**

Good guess! This means you have three of the right numbers, but only one of them is in the right place.

2 **5678—no hits!**

This is a great strategy! You can now cross out these four numbers as possibilities. And now you know one of the four has to be a zero or nine.

3 **9012—1 S, 1 F**

Two are correct, but only one's in the right spot. Look back to your previous scores for clues. Try putting the 1 and 2 back where you guessed in step 1.

4 **1290—2 F**

Only two Fish—time to eliminate some numbers. Try pairing two possibilities with numbers you know are **not** in the answer (see step 2).

I'm definitely not in the right spot...yipe!

5 9056—1 S

Only one hit. It's safe to say that either 9 or 0 is the Shark. Pick one, keeping it in the same position, and try a new combination of numbers.

6 2014—2S, 1F

From steps 3, and 4, we can see that if we use 0, both 1 and 2 cannot be in the secret number (there were only two hits in these steps). So let's try 1, but not 2, next time.

7 1034—2S, 1F

Let's try the same combination, but this time replace the 1 with the 2.

8 2034—2S, 2F

Spot on! You now know all four numbers and which two need to be switched to get the answer. (See answer on page 160.)

WIZARD'S DICE

Harry Snotter and Ron Sneezely play this spooky game with friends when they are supposed to be studying for Potions.

YOU'LL NEED

three or more players

paper

pencils

three or more dice

1 Each player draws a spider head, body, and legs on their paper, like this:

and a stick person with two fingers on each hand, and two toes on each foot, like this:

2 The shortest player decides how many dice you will use for the game: 3, 4, or 5 dice. The greater number of dice, the harder the game.

3 The tallest player goes first. Take turns following the most magical direction, clockwise.

4 The object of the game is to make an equation out of the dice roll that adds up, in any way, to the magic number eight. You can subtract, add, multiply, or divide the numbers. Each die can only be used once. You must use all the dice for each equation.

Example 1: $5+4-1 = 8$

Example 2: $(6 \times 2) - (4 \times 1) = 8$

or $(6 \times 4) \div (2+1) = 8$

(do math in brackets first)

If you can come up with an equation, you have tamed the spider. Cross out a leg from the spider body. If you cannot come up with an equation (for example, if the dice rolled are 1, 1, and 1), the spider gets a chomp out of you! Cross out one of the toes or fingers on your stick figure.

Take turns rolling the dice and crossing out spider legs or wizard digits until someone has vanquished the spider (crossed out all eight legs from the drawing). A player that loses all of his fingers and toes must sit out the next game.

Game Variations

Try playing with your equations having to add up to 10 or 24.

Make rolling "snake eyes"—two ones—an automatic lose a turn.

Roll four sixes for an "Abracadabra": you win.

ANSWERS

Page 92 Secret Message:
You're Really Smart

Page 102 Kooky Calculator:
1) Boil eels; 2) Blob; 3) Bee;
4) Goggles; 5) Solo; 6) She Lies;
7) Shoe; 8) Boss; 9) SOS; 10) Slob;
11) Loose; 12) Go, Gill; 13) Ho ho ho;
14) He big; 15) Hisses; 16) Belle;
17) Hi ho, hi ho; 18) Ill Isle

Page 104–105 Wacky Word Series:
1) 7—Each shape is a number facing
its mirror image. 2) Filled-in Circle—
The pattern shows the phases of the
moon. The next phase would be a
new moon. 3) U—These letters run
along the top row of letters on a
keyboard. 4) A, for August—These
letters are the first letters of the
months: January, February, March,
April, May, June, July… 5) K—The
list is every other letter of the
alphabet. 6) 64—Each number is
double the number before it. 7) 7
Days in a Week; 8) 52 Cards in a
Deck; 9) 12 Eggs in a Dozen; 10) 5
Fingers on a Hand; 11) 100 Cents in
a Dollar; 12) 2 Wheels on a Bike; 13)
26 Letters in the Alphabet; 14) 365
Days in a Year; 15) 360 Degrees in a
Circle; 16) 24 Hours in a Day; 17) 60
Seconds in a Minute; 18) Half-baked
idea; 19) Double or nothing; 20) Man
overboard; 21) Split personality;
22) Skinny dipping; 23) Look out
below!; 24) Mirror image; 25) Forty
winks; 26) Stinky underwear; 27)
There's a fly in my soup; 28) Rough
seas; 29) Crossword; 30) Merry-go-
round; 31) Somewhere over the
Rainbow; 32) Identical twins; 33) Read
between the lines; 34) Long-johns.

**Page 106 Gadzooks Family
Reunion:** None of the party crashers
has any hair (on top of their heads or
on their face). There are three more
party crashers (bottom left in elf hat,
man coming through window, and
boy swinging from chandelier).

**Page 108 Mischief at the Theater
Royale:** Sir Hugh Dunnit Noughtmie
stole Veronica Poopkin's diamond
necklace.

Page 114 Lost Loot Line-Up:
Stan "the man" Nitwit

**Page 122 Lady Pink's Hidden
Treasure:** 1) The starting point is
home plate of the baseball diamond.
2) Nine flip flops north takes you to
the garbage dump. 3) Clue three
takes you all the way to the bottom
right corner to the skipping rope.
4) Six flip flops north takes you to the
pail and shovel in the sand. 5) Two
flip flops northwest takes you to the
ice cream truck. 6) This clue takes
you to the tree at the bottom of the
page. 7) Nine flip flops northwest
takes you to the toy boat floating
in the pool. 8) This clue forces you
overboard into the middle of the
pool. The treasure is buried in the
middle of the pool. The colored
capital letters spell out your treasure:
DIAMOND EARRINGS

Page 125 Meet the Oddys:
1) Grandpa: My favorite band is
playing tonight at the hall. 2) Zack:
My totally cool homework is done.
3) Mama: Next stop, Main Street
Station! 4) Grandma: Would you like
the scarf when I'm done? 5) Martha: If
it's sunny soon, we can go swimming.
6) Papa: Would you like to hear
some music?

Page 126 Scenic Route Road Trip:
Map begins at Free Pass 1) South
to Lizard Lips 2) South to Last Water
Hole 3) East to Loneman's Ridge
4) East to George's Gorge 5) East
to Valley of No Rain 6) North to
Coyote's Paw 7) West to Echoing
Cavern 8) North to Witch's Brew
9) West…To California! You've
reached your destination.

**Page 129 Yolanda's Potion (mystery
ingredient):** 1) Newt 2) Broom
3) Warlock 4) Ghosts 5) Terrible
6) Magic Wand 7) Abracadabra.
The mystery ingredient is CABBAGE.

Page 148 Transformations: Cat to
Dog: cat; cot; dot; dog. Top to Hat:
top; hop; hot; hat. Give to Take: give;
gave; cave; cake; take. Read to Book:
read; rear; bear; boar; boor; book.
Fish to Hook: fish; fist; mist; mast;
mask; mark; dark; dork; cork; cook;
hook. Book to Worm: book; cook;
cork; core; care; ware; warm; worm.

Page 156 Sharks and Fish:
The mystery number is 3024.